W9-CID-458

Social Work
and Alzheimer's Disease

Practice Issues With
Victims and Their Families

Social Work and Alzheimer's Disease

Practice Issues With Victims and Their Families

Rose Dobrof
Editor

The Haworth Press
New York • London

Social Work and Alzheimer's Disease: Practice Issues With Victims and Their Families has also been published as *Journal of Gerontological Social Work,* Volume 9, Number 2, Winter 1985/86.

The Haworth Press, Inc., 28 East 22 Street, New York, NY 10010-6194
EUROSPAN/Haworth, 3 Henrietta Street, London WC2E 8LU England

Library of Congress Cataloging-in-Publication Data
Main entry under title:

Social work and Alzheimer's disease.

"Has also been published as Journal of gerontological social work, volume 9, number 2, winter 1985/86"—T. p. verso.
Includes bibliographies.
1. Medical social work—United States—Addresses, essays, lectures. 2. Presenile dementia—Addresses, essays, lectures. 3. Social work with the aged—United States—Addresses, essays, lectures. I. Dobrof, Rose
HV687.5.U5S63 1985   362.6   85-22026
ISBN 0-86656-402-0

Social Work and Alzheimer's Disease: Practice Issues With Victims and Their Families

Journal of Gerontological Social Work
Volume 9, Number 2

CONTENTS

WORLD OF PRACTICE

BOOK REVIEWS

Acknowledgements

This study was initiated while I was a Fulbright fellow in Australia in 1983. The original conceptualization of the research and most of the Australian data collection were sponsored by this fellowship and were undertaken during my four-month stay at the Australian National University's Research School for Social Sciences, Ageing and the Family Project. Subsequent analysis, data collection and writing took place after I returned to Johns Hopkins and was sponsored by a grant from the Australian Council on the Ageing.

I owe a major debt of gratitude to a very large number of Australian colleagues who generously gave much time and effort to helping me with this project: at the Ageing and the Family Project—Diane Gibson, Don Rowland, and Susan Wells; at the Australian Bureau of Statistics—Earle McKay, Bruce Illingsworth, and Fred Dawes; at the Social Welfare Policy Secretariat—Marie Coleman, Daryl Dixon, John Elias, and Nick Swain; at the Policy Coordination Unit, Claudia Thame; at the Department of Health—Alan Doobov and Peter Fisher; at the Department of Social Security—Ann Brennan, Mary Scott, and John Lloyd; at Westmead Hospital—Gary Andrews and Ann Davidson; at Mount Royal Hospital—Anna Howe; at the University of New South Wales—Adam Graycar; at Australian National University—Ken Foreman and Mike Tatchell.

Special thanks are also due to Mr. Bruce Farrer of the Australian American Educational Foundation for his help and support during my residence in Australia, Hal Kendig, Coordinator of the Ageing and the Family Project, who was my host at ANU, and to John Hemer and Sid Sax of the Project who were always ready to discuss and re-discuss the issues.

A number of my Australian and American colleagues have been of enormous help to me over the several years it has taken to produce this report: Verdon Staines (Social Welfare Policy Secretariat); Roger Jones (Social Science Data Archive, ANU); Victor Minichiello (Ageing and the Family Project, ANU); Judy Feder and Bill Scanlon (Georgetown University); Marilyn Moon (The Urban Institute), and Susan Kane (Johns Hopkins University). Marie Danna patiently and carefully typed the manuscript.

One final note. Every aspect of my connection to Australia through this research, from the exchange of ideas it has generated to the lifelong friendships it has allowed me to form, might be described as a once in a lifetime experience. I hope it is not.

Sandra J. Newman
Johns Hopkins University
Institute for Policy Studies

FROM THE EDITOR

In one sense, there is an irony in our dedication of an entire issue of the Journal to the subject of *Social Work and Alzheimer's Disease: Practice Issues With Victims and Their Families.* The irony can be fully appreciated if one reviews the social work literature of the 20th century: nomenclature has changed; the knowledge base and the repertoire of treatment modalities and intervention skills have increased remarkably; more is known about incidence and prevalence of Senile Dementia; Alzheimer's is still not curable, but research which offers promise is being conducted at major medical centers across the land. The public knows about Alzheimer's: it is the subject of movies, television specials, and feature articles in newspapers and magazines. And health and social service agencies have responded: indeed, as the reader will see, this issue includes a number of articles reporting on the design of new programs and approaches.

So there is much that is new, yet the irony is that demented old people and social workers are not strangers to each other. You can go as far back as the writings of Jane Addams and other founders of the American settlement house movement or to early reports with old people "in their dotage." The social workers who carried Old Age Assistance case loads after the passage of the Social Security Act; medical social workers in general hospitals; the social service workers in the Veterans Administration; psychiatric social workers in state mental hospitals; and, of course, social workers in Homes for the Aged—all of these workers, long before Alzheimer's became known as the "Disease of the 20th Century" or was ranked as one of the four leading killers of Americans, encountered and tried to help demented older people and their families.

My own first experiences with this group were in a state mental hospital in the 1950s: they were on "the back wards" of the hospital—wards in which there was no hope, and in which the task was defined as the provision of *humane* custodial care, which meant the

1

prevention of bedsores and contractures; the reduction, through the use of an experimental new drug called Thorazine of agitated or aggressive behavior; and the tolerance of bizarre behavior—so long as the behavior posed no threat to the patient or other patients or the staff. Professional social workers, then in scarce supply, were not assigned to the back wards; they were to work with patients for whom there was the possibility of recovery.

But my assignment, as the first group worker on the staff, was to establish a group for the families of newly admitted patients. And painfully do I remember some of the members of that group: the handsome, respectable, proud man in his 70s who at the end of his rope had brought his wife to the hospital. He could no longer "handle" her at home; the much maligned and greatly feared state mental hospital was the only place which would accept her.

My memory is that the diagnosis was "hardening of the arteries," and the old man understood that it was not his fault, nor was it divine retribution. But he had endured so much in the months before he finally brought her to us, and the disease had robbed him of the wife he so clearly adored. And for her "to end up" in a state mental hospital, the knowledge that after 50 years of married life, he could not save her from this fate—this was the source of his agony.

There were others like him; wives worn out by their efforts to keep their husbands at home; children, married with their own families, not able to understand what happened to their proud self-reliant parents. It was called "hardening of the arteries" or "senility," and it was incurable, and our task as social workers was to comfort the families; to help them find solace in the company of the similarly afflicted; to try to make the institution seem less forbidding and terrible.

And then in the 1960s, in a Home for the Aged, we learned from Alvin Goldfarb to call the condition "chronic Brain Syndrome," and we learned that although there was still no cure, *humane* custodial care meant more than simply the prevention of bedsores, contractures, and disturbed and disturbing behavior. We learned about the importance of accurate diagnosis and about the design of a supportive environment. We learned that physicians, nurses, social workers, occupational therapists and others could help people make maximum use of remaining resources (Dr. Goldfarb called this "minimizing functional disability in excess of the organicity"). We learned that particularly early in the course of the disease, people responded to what was happening to them in sorrow, anger, and fear and that there were anodynes to this pain. We learned how little we knew; how much there was to learn; how much was still unknown. And, of course, we learned that just as had been true at the mental hospital, so also here, the families needed our understanding, empathy, compassion, and help.

And now it is the mid 1980s, and this issue reflects the upsurge of interest in Senile Dementia/Alzheimer's Type; the increasingly rich practice experience of social workers in a variety of settings; and the commitment of social workers to the task of deepening their knowledge base and refining their practice skills—a commitment firmly embedded in the professional and personal values and ethics of the social workers dedicated to service to this group. You see, I hope, the irony: the disease is not new, nor is social work practice with the demented aged new. We build today on a long and honorable tradition in our profession. We hope this volume will be both faithful to that tradition, and a contribution to the work of the present and future.

Rose Dobrof
Editor

Special Nursing Home Units for Residents With Primary Degenerative Dementia: Alzheimer's Disease

Nancy R. Peppard

INTRODUCTION

It is estimated that chronic dementing syndromes, regardless of etiology, are present in 50%-70% of all residents in nursing homes today (DHHS, 1980; Besdine, 1978). The incidence of dementia is significantly higher in females than males (Neuman & Cohn, 1978). Moreover, the prevalence is for females to live longer with the syndrome than males. Since the instance of dementia increases with age (but as yet is not directly known to be concomitant of the aging process), the majority of persons residing in an extended care facility with this diagnosis can be profiled as female, over 75, single with infrequent or non-existant family or extended family ties. This presents compounding challenges for monitoring proper care and management of this population.

As our society continues to age at a proportionately high rate, the instance of persons presenting some form of dementia will dramatically increase. Presently, the nursing home industry is inadequately prepared to meet the challenge. The mental deterioration and eventual physical decline of persons with one or more of the dementing syndromes tend to confound the medical and psychosocial care provided to this population in an extended care setting. "Confused" residents are too frequently labeled "problem behaviors" or "difficult to manage." Ironically, the confusion lies more in the professional care provider's lack of knowledge and under-

Nancy R. Peppard is President of Alzheimer Care Management Systems, 864 Azalea Drive, PO Box 10243, Rockville, MD 20850.

© 1986 by The Haworth Press, Inc. All rights reserved.

5

standing, and less in the victim. Consequently it has been suggested (Burnside, 1981; Gunter & Miller, 1977) that not enough is being done to understand and meet the needs of this tragic group of older persons.

Perhaps due to the fact that there are no effective treatments (Eisdorfer & Stotsky, 1977; Goldfarb, et al., 1972; Zarit, 1980) for dementia, the primary focus of attention of professionals and paraprofessionals has been directed in one of two areas: bio-medical research looking for a cause and cure or psycho-social research examining the burden of care on the families. A major factor in this equation has been overlooked, and that is the victim themselves. Certainly the time has come for us to equalize our approach and recognize that counseling and supporting families will be more effective if we also offer insight for all caregivers (both families and extended care providers) through the study and development of dementia management techniques. Appropriate patient management techniques lighten the burden of the caregiver and restore some measure of dignity to the individual.

Various terms are used freely and interchangably today when discussing the vast array of psychologic or behavioral signs and symptoms that have been classified as Organic Brain Syndromes (OBS). Those terms include confusion, senility, pre-senile dementia, cognitive impairment, and disorientation. For the purposes of this article all individuals with Primary Degenerative Dementia (PDD) and related irreversible disorders will be grouped under the umbrella of Alzheimer's Disease.

PROGRAM DESIGN

How can we provide proper care and management for Alzheimer victims within a nursing home setting while remaining supportive of both family and staff? The program described herein, a special unit for Alzheimer residents, we developed in response to this question. What follows is a program that has evolved over a period of three years and is now in use in a number of nursing homes throughout the country. It is important to note that in the development of special units or special programs the basic design here presented is meant as a guide. Individualized programs must be designed and developed in each nursing home to take account of geographic, ethnic, and cultural differences as well as the physical design of the nursing home and its resources.

Many considerations have to be taken into account when developing a segregated unit for Alzheimer residents. Is it better to separate the confused from the cognitively well? What type of staff is required, in terms of personalities, ability, and numbers? How should training be designed and conducted? Should the resident programs remain similar to those offered daily within the institution or should they be specialized? What type of decor is most appropriate? These and countless other questions were taken into consideration when planning the initial unit.

To resolve these questions, a community advisory panel was assembled consisting of professionals (the clinical director of a Veteran's Hospital, an occupational therapist, a licensed clinical social worker, and a hospital discharge planner/RN); paraprofessionals (activity director, nurse's assistant, housekeeping), and nursing home administration (the Administrator, Director of Nursing, and dietician). Goals were established and a design formulated to create a wholistic environment (or milieu) that would allow behavior management techniques appropriate to individual and group needs and abilities. Specifically, we sought:

— To recognize each resident with dementia as a unique individual with needs, desires, and abilities;
— To select staff whose skills, creativity, personality, and interpersonal abilities were consistent with the variety of challenges presented by individuals with dementing illness;
— To train all unit staff members on the normal aging process, the dementias, and patient and personal management techniques;
— To provide staff and families with support in the form of group and individual counseling in order that each may be recognized and affirmed in sharing their feelings, techniques, experience, and knowledge;
— To integrate the community into the planning and continuation of the program.

An eighteen bed unit was chosen as the proper size to begin a unit. A major goal of the unit concept is to create a milieu that is conducive to reducing over- or understimulation. Highly textured, pastel-contrasted, sound absorbant materials were chosen. High glare floors, florescent lighting, and "wild" or busy patterns on wallcoverings were eliminated. Residents of the unit each select their own personal identification "label." Each label has its own distinctive design and color, i.e., a triangle, leaf, or half-moon, and is consistent on all items relating to the resident. Learning the name of the shape of the label is unimportant; recognition of shape is the goal. By affording the resident a degree of control in chosing the shape there remains a sense of ownership and continued identity with the shape long after other cues have ceased purposefulness. It is highly desirable to have residents in double or triple bedded rooms. Private rooms increase isolation, increase withdrawal and hasten functional decline. Each resident room includes an individual's "bio-board" on the wall outside of the room. The bio-board includes the name of the resident, a picture of them when they were "well," and a brief biography of their life-time achievements. The over-all atmosphere on the unit is stress-reduced, consistent, and purposefully active, i.e., there are continued, programmed activities available throughout the day.

RESIDENTS

There are many elderly people today being inaccurately burdened with the label of Alzheimer's by family members and other laypersons without any medical diagnosis. A proportion of these people—10%-15%—present symptoms of confusion as a result of a **treatable** organic condition. In order to safeguard against inappropriate admission to the unit, the admission criteria includes a complete neurological assessment with a diagnosis of Alzheimer's or a related irreversible dementia by a neurologist. Each individual is also assessed by thorough review of information gathered from medical reports, hospital records, and extensive interviews with family members and/or the significant caregiver. Family information is gathered on an assessment tool that includes the patient's social and psychological history as well as recent personal history such as "What side of the bed does the resident normally get out on?"; "Does the resident have an alarm clock next to his/her bed? If so, what type is it?", etc. After admission, a detailed care plan is developed in which all disciplines (nursing, dietary, activities, social services, nurse's assistants, volunteers, and housekeeping) are included. Care plan meetings are held each week thereafter to monitor any change in each resident. The aides are in an especially crucial position to report behavioral changes, rate behavior management techniques, and try new methods. It is important to note that not all persons with Alzheimer's Disease or a related dementia are appropriate for special units. The level of severity of the disease must be established at the outset in order to prevent premature admission to a segregated unit, or to retain a person on a unit beyond its beneficiality.

It is crucial to have well thought out discharge plans for residents when they are no longer cognitively suited to special programming. It is important for the resident in terms of transfer trauma, but it is particularly important to work closely with the families at this stage. It is at this point that the family recognizes that the final phase of the disease is close at hand. Death is imminent. Hope is gone. Family members require acutely sensitive counseling at this point.

Most Alzheimer special care units are not beginning with 18-20 new beds. Therefore, it is necessary to assess present nursing home population for the most appropriate candidates for the unit. The same admission criteria is used for current nursing home residents as for new admissions. Reisberg's (1982) "Global Deterioration Scale for Primary Degenerative Dementia" is used to establish markers for resident appropriateness. The scale consists of seven stages which range from Stage 1, "No Cognitive Decline" to Stage 7, "Very Severe Cognitive Decline." Stage 4, 5, and 6 are chosen as those which describe disease manifestations most appropriate for the program. Stage 4 is "Moderate Cognitive Decline" which describes the late confusional stage. At this point, victims can no longer perform complex tasks accurately. However, they are still able to perform activities of daily living (ADL) with little assistance. At Stage 6, victim's are largely unaware of all recent events and experiences in their lives. They retain sporadic and occasionally inaccurate knowledge of their past and remain unaware of their surroundings. They require substantial assistance with ADLs and become incontinent.

Although the percentages vary with discharge and admissions, on average, 28% of the residents on a unit have a diagnosis of Alzheimer's, 33% Multi-Infarct Dementia, and the remainder a generic diagnosis of "senile dementia." The median age averages 69.

DAILY ACTIVITIES AND CARE

Daily activities are specially designed to be appropriate to the level of each resident participant. Upon admission the activity and social service directors assess each new resident's capabilities and tolerances. Then the resident is assigned to a group of not more than six other individuals with similar abilities. Each day's shedule is similar but not rigid. For instance, activities of daily living (ADL) are normally conducted at specific times each day within the nursing home. For the dementia residents the "normal" timetable is adjustable to suit the resident's timetable upon admission. This significantly reduces transfer trauma. It is later adjusted to be more consistent with the units normal schedule. Incontinent residents are toileted every two hours and kept on a strict hydration program. Restraints are minimal and considered a last resort. With the cooperation of the residents' physician, psychotrophic drugs have been reduced or eliminated. At meals residents are encouraged to socialize and be as independent as possible. Seating at a kidney-shaped or U-shaped table is more appropriate, especially for persons who require assistance with eating. The U-shaped tables are also ideally suited for activities since the instructor can assist from in front of the resident instead of from behind. The presentation of food in terms of amounts and number of choices presented to the resident is reduced. Appropriate dishware patterns, design, and color as well as the overall dining room environment are key to successful mealtimes.

The time between meals and after dinner is segmented into 20-30 minute intervals that alternate between cognitive and exercise periods. Residents are classified and grouped according to their ability; not all resident's participate in all activities throughout the day, however, each person is encouraged to engage in at least three to four activities per day. Skills and previously unknown abilities surface which never cease to amaze the staff. Daily activities have had a dramatic, positive impact on wandering and nighttime wakefulness. Perhaps the most meaningful activities, in terms of monitoring the residents' progression, are self-portraits and topical poems done on a monthly basis. They are visable evidence of how each resident is perceiving the world and themselves.

STAFF

The staff are primarily selected from existing staff who express a desire to participate in the program. Qualities that are considered include: proficiency in present duties; a calm, resilient personality; creative ability to act appropriately even in the face of catastrophic reaction; and good interpersonal skills. A part-time program coordinator and activity aide are also on staff. The staff to resident ratio is 1:5.

The initial concerns of staff center on the fact that they do not rotate off of the unit. Consistency is of paramount importance. Not rotating lead staff to be concerned about "burn-out" from the stress of providing daily care to cognitively impaired individuals. This concern is addressed by explaining the entire unit concept of specialization, training, modification of traditional staff roles and the weekly inclusion of staff support sessions. In other words, the "professionalization" of staff.

TRAINING

Training is conducted at three different levels and includes everyone who interacts on the unit. Level One is for the professional staff (RNs, LPNs, OTs, PTs, Social Service, Activities, Speech). Staff is taken through a program detailing the normal aging process, abnormal aging, and in-depth dementia training which covers etiology, care, and management techniques. Level Two is for the paraprofessional staff, focusing primarily on the aides. They are given the same material as the professional staff but at a less technical level. Level Three is for the remainder of the staff (dietary, maintenance, laundry, and housekeeping). They are given a basic understanding of the goals of the unit, what they may anticipate when in contact with a dementia victim and how they should conduct themselves in relations to the residents, staff, and family. With the exception of Level Three, all trainees are instructed in stress reducing techniques, death and dying issues, and provided ongoing training and support groups.

FAMILY INVOLVEMENT

Placing a family member in a nursing home is a wrenching experience, but especially for Alzheimer families. Therefore, family members are encouraged to spend as much time as they desire on the unit. This is beneficial for the family in "letting go." On the other hand, their active participation with the staff help staff learn the idiosyncrasies of the individual resident which enables staff to provide better and more knowledgeable care. In addition to the family's direct involvement, the social service department provide one-on-one counseling whenever needed. Families are encouraged to become involved with groups like ADRDA so as to begin rebuilding a community network of relationships and supports that may have dwindled in caring for their family member at home. And, perhaps the greatest extra benefit of developing a positive rapport with the families for the nursing home is that they become active, dependable and creative volunteers.

The initial concern of some families upon hearing of a segregated unit is that their relative will be "warehoused" away from the rest of the population and not afforded "normal" activities and social services. These concerns are quickly dispelled by a quality unit and staff attention to needs and concerns.

EVALUATION

The initial program's purpose was to gain experience with training needs, management techniques, and family support. It was not a formal research effort. No attempt was made to formally assess the outcome through tests. However, through experience, common sense, and some trial and error methods a valuable, proven method of care has been developed that is cost effective, meaningful to residents, their families, and rewarding to the staff. Observation of residents reveals improvement or maintenance in terms of interaction, functional level, and disposition. Staff meet formidable challenges and achieve monumental success, both with the residents, their families, and in terms of job satisfaction. Staff report a high sense of satisfaction in being able to grow beyond their traditional functions. Families report a greater sense of ease in letting go of guilt, in being able to remain involved in their relatives care while resuming their own lives, and in knowing that their relatives are being cared for by a knowledgable, caring staff.

RECOMMENDATIONS

Based on the successful evolution of this program, it appears that specific training and support result in high quality, wholistic patient care; development of effective behavioral management techniques for patients previously labeled "difficult"; and increased job satisfaction for staff (in particular, aides) resulting in low turnover. Special care units for demented residents may not be appropriate in all institutions. However, a comparable investment in staff training, support and programming can be demonstrated to improve care of dementia patients in any setting.

REFERENCES

Besdine, R. W., 1978. "Treatable Dementia in Elderly" Task Force Draft. National Institute on Aging.

Burnside, I. M., 1981. Nursing and the Aged. New York: McGraw-Hill.

DHHS, 1980. "NIA Studies Causes of Alzheimer's Disease" in Special Report on Aging. Washington, DC: NIH Publication No. 80-2135, pp. 16-18.

Eisdorfer, C. and Stotky, B. A., 1977. "Intervention, Treatment and Rehabilitation of Psychiatric Disorders" in Handbook of the Psychology of Aging, edited by James Birren and K. Warner Schaie. New York: Van Nostrand Reinhold.

Goldfarb, A. E., Hochstadt, N., Jacobson, J. H., Weistein, E. A., 1972. "Hyperbaric Oxygen Treatment of Organic Mental Syndrome in Aged Patients," Journal of Gerontology, 27, 212-217.

Gunter, L. M. and Miller, J. C., 1977. "Toward a Nursing Gerontology," Nurs Res, 26(3): 208-221.

Klettner, S. J., 1979. "Hospital Design is Geared Toward Patient with Sensory Impairment," AIA Journal, February, pp. 104-105.

Neuman, M. A. and Cohn, R., 1978. "Epidemiological Approach to Questions of Identity of Alzheimer's and Senile Brain Disease: A Proposal" in Alzheimer's Disease: Senile Dementia and Related Disorders, edited by R. Katzman, R. Terry and K. Bick. New York: Raven Press, pp. 27-34.

Reisberg, B., Ferris, S. H., DeLeon, M. J. and Crook, T. 1982. "The Global Deterioration Scale of Assessment of Primary Degenerative Dementia," American Journal of Psychiatry, 139:9, pp. 1136-1139, September.

Zarit, S. H., 1980. Aging and Mental Disorders. New York: The Free Press.

Social Work Groups With Institutionalized Alzheimer's Disease Victims

Betsy Carey, ACSW
Shannon S. Hansen, BA

ABSTRACT. Description of groupwork experience on the Alzheimer's Unit at the Dallas Home for Jewish Aged. It has been found that through this group interaction a greater sense of belonging and togetherness develop that may be more important than the actual content of the group session. Suggestions for dealing with behavior problems, the impact of the environment, the problems with evaluation and two successful groups are discussed with the intent of guiding other group leaders in working with this population.

INTRODUCTION

While the recent surge of information on the symptoms and behavior of Alzheimer's Disease sufferers is enlightening for families groping for answers to management problems at home, the same information is creating problems for some practitioners. The list of precautions for dealing with this population is so extensive that many day care centers and long term care facilities continue to deny admission to Alzheimer's Disease patients. Those facilities that allow participation will find little beyond the precautions to guide them in the development of therapeutic interventions. The word is out that people with Alzheimer's Disease can be dangerous at worst, and unpredictable at best. For the safety of the majority a nontreat-

---

Betsy Carey and Shannon S. Hansen are Social Workers at the Dallas Home for Jewish Aged, 2525 Centervill Road, Dallas, TX 75228.

15

ment policy may be established by a well-meaning institution's administration. Beyond safety, another question nagging those responsible for the allocation of limited staff to resident support tasks is why bother with the memory impaired population? They can't remember; therefore, they don't benefit from any intervention.

In any discussion of groups of persons with Alzheimer's Disease, it is important to emphasize from the outset that the disease does not reduce each victim to one definable type. Every person continues as an individual with varied strengths and deficits. Each has the capacity to contribute in a distinct manner, regardless of the similarity of his/her diagnosis with another individual. A group leader will constantly be reminded of the differences between people, rather than their sameness.

What we would like to demonstrate in this article is the value of social work groups with confused elderly nursing home residents. We will present ideas available from the literature and our own experience with groupwork at the Dallas Home for Jewish Aged. Two successful groups will be presented and discussed with the intent of guiding other group leaders. Suggestions for dealing with behavior problems will be offered. The impact the environment has on any group will be reviewed and issues surrounding evaluation efforts will be explored.

SOCIAL WORK THROUGH GROUPS

Social work and other health professionals have successfully employed group work techniques with the elderly for years (Shore, 1952; Burnside, 1978). While leading a group of confused residents involves a unique set of implementation tasks, the same universal goals for participation are established: increased self esteem; increased stimulation through interaction; improved group social skills. Cook (1984) found in her reminiscence groups of confused elderly that the group encouraged active and spontaneous participation which promoted socialization and personal contact. Group psychotherapist Maurice Linden (1953) found in his work with elderly regressed women that group intervention could increase participants' alertness, diminish their confusion, and could improve their orientation. While these would not be longitudinal goals for groups of Alzheimer's Disease patients, the leader could hope for such improvements for the duration of the group, in some participants.

GROUPS OF CONFUSED RESIDENTS

In working with groups of cognitively impaired elderly, potential success is primarily a function of the leader's expectations. Goals have to be modified toward the maintenance or maximization of function rather than the expectation of long term improvement. The value of each quality moment needs to be stressed to the leader who anticipates carry-over social skill development. If participants can interact appropriately for the duration of a structured session, one is not to be dismayed that half an hour later they have returned to bickering over territorial rights to a chair.

Unlike groups of intact older people, the confused are generally more passive in their participation. The group leader must constantly solicit input. The leader should be aware of the participants' decreasing ability to think in the abstract and should therefore limit topics of discussion to tangible, concrete facts or memories. Many Alzheimer's Disease patients can be easily distracted. Using handouts which the leader expects to serve as visual aids to the discussion can end up as a disaster as group participants examine, fondle, or otherwise focus on the handout and completely lose sight of the leader. Reaction time is often slower for a confused group of elderly. As communication skills decline, individuals often become more sensitive to non-verbal cues such as facial expression and "mood." The mood of the leader or other group members is more easily transferred to the entire group, which can work in either positive or negative directions. Groupwork offers the person an opportunity to participate with peers in a shared creative activity. Through this interaction a greater sense of belonging can develop. With a cognitively impaired population, this warm feeling of "togetherness" may be more important than the actual content of the group session.

The group leader must also temper his/her expectation of response from the participants. Moods may vary from session to session. People suffering from dementia are often susceptible to dramatic mood swings regardless of all attempts to maintain a calm group environment. This is one of the few variables over which the leader has limited control. Therefore, negative responses from moody participants should not be personalized.

IMPACT OF ENVIRONMENT ON GROUPWORK

One cannot ignore the importance of the social environment in successfully implementing group sessions for the Alzheimer's

Disease resident. The social environment can be described as everything outside of one's self. Hiatt (1982) emphasizes that the more cognitively impaired the individual is, the more significance the environment takes on in coping independently and in other aspects of well being. For example, by holding group sessions in a closed, quiet area, separated from the noise or distractions of a nurses's station, one facilitates a greater attention potential in the mentally impaired person. The participant is enabled to respond more quickly and to keep track of the sequence of events.

As with other older adults, anything that can be done to support declining sensory skills such as improving lighting or acoustics can enhance memory. We have found that in working with Alzheimer's Disease residents that physically altering the environment in such a way as to say to participants, "something new and different is about to happen" aids in the success of the group. Rearranging chairs in the communal area, or moving the leader to various focal points within the same room sets the stage for a special event.

DEALING WITH BEHAVIOR PROBLEMS

Once the proper setting has been established, the group leader may have already allayed many problems. Often behavior problems are a result of the resident's frustration in communication. If the room is arranged in such a way as to provide the leader with eye contact and good acoustics, communication is facilitated, and many frustrations are dissipated.

It is essential that the leader is aware of the idiosyncrasies of each participant. One woman may refuse to enter the meeting room if no other participants are gathered, while another member may be overcome with agitation if the room looks too crowded. Wanderers should be placed close to the leader so that they can be assured of the passing time and reminded that they are an important part of the group. Sometimes the leader needs to hold the wanderers hand to keep attention and peace.

No one should be coerced into attending any group against personal wishes. Forcing attendance or any function on an Alzheimer's resident invariably produces unnecessary agitation. If one comes to a group upset, that mood is likely to disrupt others as well. Groups are not for everyone. Individuals need to be respected in their choices. The leader must invite all potential participants with the understanding that each day is different for each person. Violent, antisocial people should be excluded from groups for the sake of other participants.

SOCIAL WORK GROUPS ON THE ALZHEIMER'S UNIT AT THE DALLAS HOME FOR JEWISH AGED

A thirty bed, segregated unit for mild to moderately impaired victims of Alzheimer's Disease and other related dementing illnesses is the setting for the two following groups. Social work is only one component of a multidisciplinary approach to treatment which includes Nursing, Occupational Therapy, Physical Therapy, and Recreation. Resident groupwork is only one facet of the total social work care plan. Social work groups on the unit are not utilized as psychotherapy sessions, rather they are more eclectic in nature. The groups focus on maintaining social and mental function within the setting while discussing topics relevant to participants.

Newcomer's Group

A ten-session Newcomer's Group was conducted on the unit shortly after the wing was opened. Weekly meetings were held for 30 to 45 minutes. The stated goal set forth prior to the group was to "facilitate a successful adjustment into DHJA by fostering a sense of belongingness." The objectives were:

— to provide the residents with useful information
— to give the residents an opportunity to meet other people in similar stages of adjustment
— to enable residents to gain personal insight into their situation by becoming more familiar with themselves
— to improve socialization skills by utilizing group process techniques to reinforce acceptable behaviors.

Membership. The average group size was 6.6 residents with the lowest attendance of four (the first session) and the highest of nine (the last session). Initially members were selected from the group of recently admitted residents. By the second session, people who had lived in the home for years took an interest in the group and the leader did not want to exclude them simply because they were not "new." All recently admitted residents were invited. Several declined but were encouraged to attend for the first few sessions. A written invitation was delivered to all new admissions. Participants were also reminded at dinner to attend the meeting immediately following. The leader had to strongly coax involvement and practically take people by the arm down to the meeting area until the fourth session. It was not until the eighth meeting that members appeared to remember ever having participated previously.

Content. Each session began by reviewing the names of those present. Much of the first half of the meeting usually involved greeting each other and telling of an interesting moment during the preceding week. Some people told the same significant tale each session. The leader at this point would interject unusual events that had transpired and try to generate conversation between participants. Each session had a theme: hobbies, career, first dates, birthplace, etc. The purpose of this was to present non-threatening topics which would bring out information on each individual. The groups were lighthearted and enjoyable. The emphasis was on interaction among participants.

Evaluation. Evaluation is very difficult in a memory impaired population. The standard bases for assessment such as memory of significant factors, information gained and utilized, cannot be employed. Issues beyond memory of the event need to be subjectively analyzed.

Participants in the Newcomer's Group were interviewed within three weeks following the final session. The evaluation was to determine (1) if the participants had any memory of participating in the groups; (2) if the participant was beginning to feel comfortable at the DHJA; and (3) if the participant felt the group assisted in the adjustment.

Five of the seven interviewed said they remembered attending the group. The two women who did not remember ever participating were each 100% active. However, both stated that they felt comfortable in the nursing home. While neither remembered participating in the groups, their level of interaction at individual sessions was very high.

There were five other interviews with members who stated that they remembered participating. Three felt the groups had been worthwhile and the other two had mixed feelings about its value. For example, Mrs. W's evaluation was a reflection of her negative participation. She invariably complained when asked to attend but remarkably she was also 100% active. Mrs. W always treated the sessions as though she were pariticipating in a ladies service auxiliary. She wanted to "vote on ideas" whenever possible. In early groups she was the first to criticize if someone went off on a tangent. Near the end of the series her group skills seemed more appropriate and her tolerance toward other participants increased during the meeting.

Mrs. C also had some ambivalent feelings about the group. Her reaction was indicative of the fact that she had always been a loner and had never been group oriented. She attended out of deference to the leader but did not feel she benefited from participation. This feeling in her evaluation accurately depicts the role of passive observer she assumed during each group.

Two of the three positive evaluations came from women who assumed leadership positions during many sessions. Mrs. P was always ebullient at the Newcomer's Group and was equally rosy for the evaluation. She was not a newcomer but enjoyed the forum for her pleasantries. She regularly helped lift the spirits of others which was a different role than she assumed outside of the group.

Mrs. S began asserting a leadership role which she has maintained in other capacities since the group. She was the most articulate member of the group and her peers allowed her to take control. This was a new responsibility for her because she had come to the Alzheimer's Unit from another apartment where her social inadequacies were more pronounced in comparison to those residents. In this secure structure, she rose to the occasion. She actively participated in the groups and solicited input from others. When asked if the meetings were helpful to her adjustment she commented, "I always liked to attend the meetings because people let their hair down . . . it was worthwhile because I got to know some people in a small group." This woman still does not know the name of her table mates in the dining room but she did function at a very high level in this group.

The final positive evaluation came from Mrs. D who was having increasing difficulty expressing herself verbally. Mrs. D was not interested in participating but yielded to the leader's persuasion once and came without being pushed thereafter. During the sessions the other participants were patient as Mrs. D struggled to say what was on her mind and she was willing to try to speak. However, as people left the group Mrs. D would again be chastised if she was unable to communicate clearly or quickly enough for the other women. This transformation was apparent to Mrs. D and she mentioned it during the evaluation. Why did she attend? "We talked about ideas, things we did, got acquainted, good for the meeting then Phew! That was it!"

The phenomenon Mrs. D is describing is that the mood seemed to change from the time the group was over and the participants returned to "their" chairs in the living room. They often left arm and arm from the meeting site, got to the living room and began bickering again as though they had not spent any good natured time together previously. As a whole, the group skills of individual members improved during the sessions but as they left the meetings they returned to the same roles they maintained in the larger group. While attending the sessions they were removed from their routine environment in the living room and with leadership, they seemed to form a more democratic, extending courtesies to each other that they didn't always allow in the larger arena. Many members of the group felt a belongingness while in attendance, but this feeling seemed to dissipate as they physically removed themselves from the group setting.

Current Events Group

The Current Events group meets weekly for a one-hour period. It is the responsibility of the social worker as group leader to gather newspaper or magazine articles of current newsworthy interest. This group has met weekly since December of 1983 and is an ongoing program on the Alzheimer's Unit. "CE" was designed with two goals in mind: (1) to familiarize the individual with the current happenings and events taking place in the immediate environment, community, and world; and (2) to promote mental stimulation and awareness. The objectives were:

— to provide opportunities for residents to discuss and debate current issues, events, and newsworthy items
— to facilitate reality orientation for those residents who have been isolated or unable to keep in contact with the world around them
— to encourage residents to read newspapers or magazines or watch television news or documentaries in order to provide input during the CE class as well as become informed about newsworthy items on a daily basis

— to form a cohesive group in which relationships can be established and supported in daily living.

Membership. The group is comprised of those residents who show an interest in participating or sitting in on the classes. An average of 12 people participate per session.

Content. The group leader places chairs in a circle in the dining room on the unit and invites residents to participate. Each class begins by stating the name and purpose of the group, "This is Current Events. We meet each week to discuss . . . " The leader then reads and discusses two or three articles about national or international news and ends with two or three articles of more human interest or humor. This format gives the residents an opportunity to listen and to understand the content of the group. One participant explains the format as, "we get the heavy stuff out of the way first so we can really talk later."

Evaluation. Evaluating the impact of CE has been difficult for all the reasons enumerated previously. As this is an ongoing group, no formal post-implementation evaluation has been conducted; however, we have found that group members most often do not recall attending the sessions much less relate learning anything new. Objectives three and five have therefore been proven unrealistic. Many positive aspects of group intervention have been realized. Mental stimulation and enjoyment have enhanced self-esteem and awareness. Group members can identify the leader as a person who "teaches me new things" even though they don't recall specific topics which have been "taught." Consistently as participants enter the room for the group they begin smiling and laughing. Residents that ordinarily do not speak to others compliment fellow group members for funny or insightful comments. One woman stated that if she won a million dollar lottery that she would donate all the money to the poor. The man sitting next to her complimented her on her generosity and the rest of the group followed by clapping for her.

Perhaps one of the most significant findings of the Current Events group or any other group is that distinct personality and coping styles remain even for the cognitively impaired. In Current Events there are those who assume leadership roles, those who always have a joke, those who put others at ease, those who complain, and those who are very content just to listen.

REVIEW OF GROUP GOALS

During the first year of social work groups on the Alzheimer's Unit, we have come to recognize a need to modify and review initial goals and objectives. This process of subjective review should be done continuously for all groups. Our expectation that group intervention could lead to certain improvements in the resident's activities of daily living has proven somewhat unrealistic. Objectives need to be stated in a short term, time-specific manner. One needs to look for quality interaction in the world of the group rather than expect dramatic carry over to daily life.

The evaluation of the Newcomer's Group indicated that the residents who participated in the group had made a successful adjustment into DHJA. What, if any, role the newcomer's group play in that adjustment is difficult to assess. The "belongingness" feeling fostered within the small group interactions did not seem to transcend the group into the larger arena, but a sense of belongingness was fostered within the group for the time spent in the sessions. If the goal is to maximize the moment, the moments spent in the group were maximized.

The objectives of the Newcomer's Group proved to be somewhat less realistic. Overall the subjective assessment is that the goal of successful adjustment was achieved, but not because (1) the residents were provided with useful information; or because (2) the residents had gained personal insight. Both of these objectives required that the participants be capable of utilizing new information. While some individuals afflicted with dementia are able to learn and use new material, it is not going to be achieved in a once a week session for half an hour.

In the Current Events group one additional goal could be "to give an opportunity for an enjoyable experience." One should not downplay the significance of pleasure in the arena of therapeutic intervention. Laughter is still the best medicine.

CONCLUSION

In a time of limited resources, some practitioners may feel that groupwork with this population is meaningless. This feeling may stem from the lack of carry over into improved skills in daily living and due to the difficulty in quantifying progress. We have presented some examples of positive experiences with groupwork and the Alzheimer's Disease resident in a nursing home. While we have attempted formal evaluation of these programs, we feel our subjective observation is more ecologically valid. During group sessions, we have seen improved social skills, increased self esteem, alertness, and orientation.

We have also found that one cannot expect this higher level of function to be maintained outside of the group. The success of groupwork with Alzheimer's Disease residents lies in the quality of the moment. For the duration of this special time, the resident is given the right to exchange feelings on an adult level in a secure, non-threatening environment. The role of the group leader takes on greater significance as the leader's expectations of each participant helps to determine the mood and the flow of interaction. The manipulation of the physical environment toward maximization of sensory capabilities is also essential for success.

Research in this area must continue in order to fully understand the psychosocial needs of the Alzheimer's person and how these needs can be met through groups. Our experience has merely brushed the surface as the possibilities of successful groupwork with this population are endless and need to be further explored.

REFERENCES

Burnside, I. M. *Working with elderly, group process and techniques.* Belmont, CA: Duxbury, Press, 1978.

Cook, J. B. Reminiscing: How it can help confused nursing home residents. *Social Casework: The Journal of Contemporary Social Work,* 1984, *2,* 90-93.

Hiatt, L. Environmental design and mentally impaired older people. *Mentally Impaired Aging, Bridging the Gap,* American Association of Homes for the Aged, 1982.

Linden, M. E. Group psychotherapy with institutionalized senile women: Study in gerontologic human relations. *International Journal of Group Psychotherapy,* 1953, *3,* 150-170.

Shore, H. Groupwork program development in homes for the aged. *The Social Service Review,* 1952, *2,* 108-221.

A Comprehensive Approach to Working With Families of Alzheimer's Patients

Laura Cole, MSW
Karla Griffin, MS
Barbara Ruiz, LCSW

ABSTRACT. Families who care for patients with Alzheimer's disease face severe psychosocial problems. This paper presents a comprehensive approach for social work practice with such families. The use of both clinical and social interventions is recommended to assist families in managing daily activities, alleviating stress, planning for long term care and coping with the emotional sequelae of the disease. Information-giving, teaching, and advocacy are stressed as a way of providing families with the tools they need to cope with the problems of caring for someone with a chronic, degenerative condition.

INTRODUCTION

Alzheimer's Disease is a progressive neurological disorder which accounts for 50-60% of all cases of dementia (Terry & Katzman, 1983). It afflicts approximately 1.2 million-4 million Americans over the age of 40 and is the 4th leading cause of death among the aged population (Thomas, 1983). Alzheimer's disease results in radical mental deterioration that affects each person differently in terms of its duration and manifestations. It is characterized by intellectual, language, and motor impairments which lead to forgetfulness, confusion, total disability and eventually death. The average

Laura Cole, Karla Griffin, and Barbara Ruiz are affiliated with the Family Survival Project, 1736 Divsadero Street, San Francisco, CA 94115.

27

duration of the disease is approximately seven to ten years although some people have Alzheimer's for three to four years while others may live for over 15 years after its onset (Mace, 1981).

Although there are various theories regarding the cause of Alzheimer's disease, there is currently no cure (Gwyther, 1982). Alzheimer's is usually diagnosed after all other possible causes of dementia are excluded. If a complete psychosocial and neurological examination shows no psychological or other organic cause of dementia, a diagnosis of Alzheimer's disease can tentatively be made. However, a confirmed diagnosis cannot be made until the abnormal tissues and cells in the brain are examined at the time of autopsy (Terry & Katzman, 1983).

Alzheimer's disease can have profound psychological effects on all members of the family. In the early stages, when symptoms first appear or a diagnosis is made, denial is common.Families frequently express hope that the diagnosis is a mistake and that the patient will recover. This denial serves a positive purpose in protecting them against the overwhelming reality of the disease. However, if family members persist in their denial, they will have severe problems later on in coping and adjustment.

Family members may also feel a profound sense of loss, as a loved one who was once a vital person gradually loses mental, physical and social abilities. Feelings of frustration are also common because caregivers are powerless to stop or change the course of the disease. Because the disease has an unknown etiology and affects each person differently, families often experience a great deal of fear. Caregivers may fear the behavioral and financial problems that lie ahead and children are concerned that the disease may be hereditary (Gwyther, 1982).

As the disease progresses and the person becomes increasingly dependent, role adjustments in the family unit become necessary (Lezak, 1978). The spouse and children must assume the role of guardian. Previously simple tasks such as money management, cooking, and driving become too difficult for an Alzheimer's patient and must therefore be turned over to the caregiver, other family member or attendant. Gradually, patients begin exhibiting many behavioral problems as a result of memory loss. Repetitive questioning, wandering, forgetfulness, paranoia and sometimes violence are all common manifestations of the disease (Mace, 1981). This behavior as well as the change in familial roles often causes anger and resentment which is followed by guilt.

Feelings of guilt are extremely common among families for a number of reasons. For example, family members may feel guilty for becoming embarrassed at the person's bizarre behavior in public. Anger at the person's inability to perform even the simplest of tasks is another source of guilt. Caregivers often suffer from unresolved guilt when they begin considering the possibility of placing a loved one in a nursing facility.

During the latter stages of the disease the Alzheimer's patient becomes totally incapacitated. At this time, families may go through a grieving period in which they mourn the loss of a loved one. However, because the patient is still living, family members often need permission to grieve the loss of a personal relationship that no longer exists (Mace, 1981).

Throughout the course of the disease, caregivers often experience depression, isolation and physical deterioration. Continual care of a demented person, without relief or positive changes, can leave caregivers feeling emotionally exhausted. Isolation compounds the problem, since the demands of 24 hour care prevent them from maintaining outside interests. As a result, it is not uncommon for caregivers to become physically ill and develop stress-related disorders. Because of the often bizarre characteristics of the disease, friends and even extended family drift away. This adds to the caregivers' loneliness and depression (Lezak, 1978). Establishing new friendships and attending occasional social functions can help minimize these feelings.

Financial and legal problems compound the difficulties of caring for an Alzheimer's patient. As the disease progresses, Alzheimer's patients become unable to manage their affairs. Actions such as signing checks, paying bills, drawing up a will and making personal medical decisions become impossible feats. At this point, it is important that these responsibilities be turned over to the caregiver or other family member. Legal steps, including making a will and obtaining a power of attorney, can be taken that will protect the interests of the Alzheimer's patient (Family Survival Project Handbook, 1981). A lawyer should be consulted on estate planning issues to ensure that the patient's affairs are in order.

If the Alzheimer's patient was the main provider, the loss of income can have a serious financial impact. The spouse is forced to bear the full burden of supporting the family. Income usually becomes limited to Social Security, pensions and investments, and savings that had originally been set aside for retirement. Added to this is the high cost of in-home or institutional care for the brain-damaged adult. When a person is in the middle or later stages of the disease, 24 hour a day care may be required. The costs of in-home care, residential or skilled nursing facilities often become the largest financial expenditure for a family (Family Survival Handbook, 1981). It should be noted that Alzheimer's patients frequently do not require the expensive nursing care provided at a skilled nursing facility. However, because of the behavioral characteristics of the disease (e.g., wandering, violent outbursts and incontinence), the lack of intermediate care facilities and the difficulty of 24 hour in-home care, many caregivers have little choice but to place their family member in a skilled nursing facility.

Whether a person with Alzheimer's disease is cared for at home or in an institution, the cost can be so great that it depletes a family's income and savings. Since there is currently little aid available to help pay for this care, many families who were previously financial-ly secure are forced to accept public assistance in the form of Medicaid and SSI (Family Survival Handbook, 1981).

This paper will present a comprehensive approach to working with families of Alzheimer's patients. The specific objective of this approach is to help family members deal most effectively with the situation by: (1) alleviating stress; (2) providing a safe environment where they can ventilate some of their feelings of anger, fear and depression; (3) educating them about the nature, symptoms and dynamics of Alzheimer's disease; (4) assisting them in decision-making, problem-solving and long term planning and; (5) linking them with other agencies and resources in the community which can provide additional support and services.

INTERVENTIONS

Because the problems faced by families of Alzheimer's patients are both psychological and social, it is essential that the social worker be knowledgeable and skilled in using a variety of interven-tions and techniques. Most families have a dual purpose in seeking help. They need concrete assistance and information about the disease and its prognosis in order to make plans and decisions for the future. At the same time, they are reaching out for the emotional support that will enable them to cope with the trauma of losing a loved one. The social worker who offers only concrete services in response to a request for help addresses only part of the problem. Likewise, the social worker who offers only counseling ignores the complex relationship between mental health and the social environment.

Appropriate interventions are both clinical and social and must be employed simultaneously. Because of the immediacy of the concerns with which most families must deal, it is important to direct interventions toward solving current problems rather than attempting to restructure personality or achieve long term behavioral change.

Clinical Interventions

Individual counseling for the primary caregiver assists in decision-making, problem-solving, and long term care planning as well as providing an opportunity for the caregiver to express feelings of frustration, grief, anger, and resentment in a supportive, non-judgemental environment. For many caregivers, simply knowing that the social worker is available to listen is enough. For others, especially those whose past relationship with the Alzheimer's patient has been problematic, more intensive therapy may be needed to sort out and resolve old feelings of anger and resentment which may surface as the patient becomes increasingly dependent on the caregiver. If not recognized, these feelings can severely affect the caregiver's ability to cope with the stress of caring for the patient. If the caregiver feels guilty about such feelings, s/he may attempt to alleviate guilt by taking on too much responsibility and refusing or sabotaging all offers of assistance. The eventual outcome of this behavior is a breakdown of the caregiver's own mental and physical health which can result in premature placement of the patient in an institution. A less common but more critical result of failure to recognize the caregiver's feelings is patient abuse or neglect.

Individual counseling is also helpful to caregivers in learning how to manage some of the more difficult behavioral and physical manifestations of the disease. In dealing with these issues, the social worker assumes a teaching role, giving direct advice and instruction. In cases where physical symptoms present problems, nursing consultation may be needed. Family education groups which focus on management techniques can be a valuable supplement to individual problem-solving. Teaching patient management greatly increases caregiver's abilities and self-confidence in managing the patient at home, and provides them with a means to control the amount of stress involved in living with an Alzheimer's patient.

In most cases, clinical interventions should be focused on enhancing caregivers' abilities to cope with the daily tasks of caring for a brain-damaged adult. A thorough assessment of caregivers' ego strengths and previous coping skills is an essential element in assisting them in adapting to the constantly changing demands of caregiving. Supportive interventions which bolster their self-confidence and self-esteem are especially effective as many caregivers question whether they are doing the "right thing." Giving caregivers permission to take care of themselves as well as the patient is also important in helping them maintain as normal a life style as possible.

In cases where there are a number of family members involved in the patient's care, family counseling can be an effective way to facilitate decision making and prevent conflict from developing over such issues as placement and finances. In counseling sessions, each family member has an opportunity to express their feelings and present their ideas about what is best for the patient as well as hear what others in the family are feeling and thinking. Family sessions frequently include the adult children of the elderly patient. This can present special problems for the social worker. There may be a great disparity between the siblings, not only in their ideas of appropriate care but also in their abilities to provide financial and emotional support to the caregiver. In dealing with the inevitable conflict that results from such disparity, it is important that the social worker keep in mind that the primary concern is the welfare of the patient and caregiver, not the relationships between other family members. At the same time, attention must be paid to these relationships if the family unit is to be able to reach workable solutions to problems.

Another area of frequent conflict arises when adult children disagree with parents over the issue of what constitutes appropriate care. Children tend to be concerned with issues of safety while their elderly parents want to maintain their independence as long as possible even if doing so involves some risk. Adult children may see this striving for independence as proof of their parents inability to make rational decisions. For the social worker attempting to resolve such conflicts, client self-determination must be weighed against the possible dangers that an Alzheimer's patient may present to himself or others. If the patient is wandering out of the house and becoming lost, continuing to drive, or using potentially dangerous appliances without supervision, the caregiver should be encouraged to consider taking more restrictive measures than might be necessary under less extreme circumstances.

Short term small group therapy for caregivers can be an effective way of dealing with some of the more difficult clinical issues. Caregivers often have conflicting feelings about the patient, the caregiving role, and the many changes in their lives which result from a diagnosis of Alzheimer's disease. The therapy group provides an environment where such feelings can be brought into the open, discussed with others, and resolved, thereby enhancing the caregivers' ability to problem-solve on a concrete level. Group members provide each other with feedback from a variety of perspectives and, through the dynamic interaction of group members, caregivers are able to re-examine their motivations and expectations. A primary role for the social worker in such a group is to maintain a focus on improving daily functioning and problem solving abilities rather than allowing the group to become an arena for resolving unrelated, longstanding conflicts. Referral to long term individual or group therapy may be needed in some cases.

Throughout the course of the disease, support groups for caregivers and family members are an important resource. Some caregivers may prefer to participate in a support group rather than to attend formal group therapy. Support groups complement traditional clinical interventions and expand services available to a very needy group.

The central theme of an Alzheimer's caregiver support group is shared experience. Caregivers frequently feel isolated and believe that no one else understands their feelings of loss. A support group not only reduces isolation and validates feeling, but also allows caregivers to become helpers and receivers of help simultaneously. Recognizing the enormity of the task and exploring alternative methods of problem-solving eases feelings of inadequacy and self blame and allows caregivers to take control of what may have been perceived as an overwhelming situation. Outcomes of the support group include adaptive coping through emotional support, information and guidance. As the group becomes more cohesive, informational needs are replaced by sharing personal needs and feelings. Leadership sometimes emerges as the members gain confidence in their abilities to help each other.

Support groups also provide the continuity needed to follow the course of an often lengthy illness through many stages. For the caregiver, the support group is a forum for developing coping strategies and adapting to the many stressful changes involved in chronic illness.

Social Interventions

In addition to specific clinical interventions, there are a variety of social interventions which can be used to assist caregivers. Respite care is an excellent way of relieving stress and allowing caregivers to maintain some of their normal social or recreational activities outside the home. Day programs can be used to provide respite as well as stimulation and socialization for the patient. In cases where the patient is not appropriate for a day program, in-home respite may be used. Whichever type of respite is deemed more appropriate, it is important to remember that the Alzheimer's patient has difficulty adapting. Changes should be made slowly and an initial adjustment period is usually needed. This adjustment period may be difficult for caregivers as well. Many people have problems accepting help and may worry that their loved one will not be properly cared for by outsiders. The social worker needs to be especially supportive during these times of transition.

Legal concerns are another common source of anxiety, especially for elderly women, who may have little experience with such matters. These issues are usually easily resolved if there is access to an attorney who is knowledgeable and sensitive. Advance planning can frequently solve whatever problems exist and allows families to turn their attention to other issues. Unfortunately, financial problems present more difficulties and may continue to plague families throughout the course of the disease. There is little affordable care available for the patient. Low cost, in-home respite programs or day care programs usually have long waiting lists and nursing home care is too expensive for most families to consider on a private pay basis. For many middle income families, life savings can be wiped out in a few short years. Long term financial planning can help solve some of these problems. By planning ahead families can budget their money wisely, protect their assets, and anticipate future care needs and costs.

Throughout the course of working with families and caregivers, it is important to emphasize long term care planning as a strategy for making a frightening situation somewhat more manageable. In this way, families will be able to anticipate problems and plan solutions before crises develop. Through the planning process, families are able to evaluate all the options available to them in caring for the patient and for themselves.

Part of long term care planning includes giving families accurate medical information about Alzheimer's disease. Such information plays a key role in their comprehension and acceptance of the diagnosis. Since it is not currently possible to diagnose Alzheimer's disease with 100% accuracy prior to autopsy, many questions and doubts must be addressed. Information about the subtle characteristics of the early stages, the progress of the disease, and the corresponding level of care required will reduce their fears, help them cope, and anticipate changes. If no diagnosis has been made, such information may encourage families to seek a complete neurological evaluation to rule out other reversible causes of dementia. Pamphlets, books, and journal articles about Alzheimer's disease can supplement the social worker's personal interactions with caregivers.

Centralized access to information about community resources through someone familiar with the needs of the Alzheimer's patient will assist family decision-making. The social worker can help define types of services available and help caregivers identify and assess their needs. Since resources for long term care are often limited and unaffordable, a creative approach to identifying resources will provide more options for the caregivers. Many communities have Alzheimer's groups which maintain lists of resources. Linkage with these groups will expand the social worker's knowledge about Alzheimer's disease, family caregiving intervention, and the availability of services. Other professional affiliations in long term care, information and referral, and clinical practice will enrich the skills needed to advise and guide caregivers.

Advocacy skills should be used throughout the counseling process. Individual advocacy encourages caregivers to regain control and adapt to changing circumstances. Within a group, advocacy takes the form of mutual support and reassurance. Legislative advocacy may also result from group efforts as members provide testimony and organize letter-writing campaigns in support of additional services. The personal and political empowerment of family caregivers is an important objective of the counseling process in order to direct anger outward toward social change.

CASE STUDY

Ms. K is a 65 year old woman whose 68 year old husband was recently diagnosed as having Alzheimer's disease. The Ks have been married 37 years and have one son and two daughters. All of them are married, have busy careers and families of their own. Mr. K is retired and Ms. K has been a housewife for most of her married life. They have a modest income from Mr. K's combined pension and social security. Ms. K was referred to a social worker at a local agency by the doctor who diagnosed her husband. Ms. K has followed through on the referral although she tells the social worker that she does not believe that there is any help for her. She feels that her situation is hopeless.

When Ms. K meets with the social worker, two of her three children accompany her, although Ms. K provides most of the information. She states that she is worried about her husband, whom she has left at home alone. Her presenting problems seem to center on behavior management issues. She states that her husband's "bizarre" behavior is driving her crazy. He wanders around the house aimlessly both during the day and at night. Ms. K seldom gets a full night's sleep since she must get up each time he does to put him back to bed. He has attempted to use the stove and started a grease fire. He is paranoid and suspicious of his wife, accusing her of stealing his possessions and mismanaging their money. He also refuses to stop driving the car although he is clearly a danger on the road. Ms. K states that her husband continues to be in excellent physical condition while her own health is deteriorating. She has arthritis and has recently developed high blood pressure. She claims that she is physically and emotionally exhausted much of the time. She feels that her husband does things simply to annoy her and she experiences great frustration in trying to explain to him why his behavior is irrational. Ms. K also states that she feels lonely and depressed much of the time as most of their old friends have drifted away. The children concur with their mother's assessment of the situation. They also express concern about their father's safety and their mother's mental and physical state. They believe that she is unable to cope with the burdens of caretaking and feel their father might be better off in a "rest home."

During the family's explanation of the problems, the social worker listens, and projects an empathetic and understanding attitude. The family is allowed to tell their story and express their feelings in their own words. Only after this is done will they be able to accept suggestions and feedback from the social worker. Since behavior seems to be a great source of stress, the social worker begins by suggesting some strategies for controlling dangerous or annoying behavior. To begin with, the social worker urges Ms. K to take the car keys away from her husband. Ms. K is reluctant to do so because she feels that the car is a "symbol of his independence." However, she realizes that his driving presents a danger to others and agrees to begin taking the necessary steps to curtail his driving. The social worker also encourages Ms. K to call her doctor to inquire about medications which might help her husband sleep through the night. The social worker further discusses the behavioral characteristics and prognosis of the disease in order to help Ms. K understand her husband's irrational behavior.

Noting how tired Ms. K looks, the social worker suggests respite care, either in-home or at a day program. She then goes on to explain to the family the different levels of in-home and out-of-home care and the costs of each. Ms. K takes this opportunity to express her wish that her husband remain at home for as long as possible. Ms. K's children are surprised to hear their mother's firm resolve to keep their father at home. Further discussion helps them to realize that they have been unaware of their mother's need to demonstrate her love and commitment to her husband by caring for him during his illness.

At this point, both of her children express their willingness to help with some of the burden of caring for their father. However, because of their responsibilities to their own children and careers, they are unable to give Ms. K as much support as she needs. The social worker suggests that Ms. K look into day programs which could provide respite for her as well as socialization and stimulation for her husband. Ms. K's daughter volunteers to help her mother make such arrangements and Ms. K, although somewhat reluctant to accept outside help, agrees to consider this option. The social worker also points out that out-of-home placement may become necessary in the future and refers the family to an attorney who can assist them in financial planning and give them information about public assistance program regulations. The social worker also suggests that the family discuss wills and conservatorships with the attorney.

Before ending this session, the social worker encourages the family to attend a support group, and offers to continue seeing Ms. K individually to assist her in dealing with her depression and grief. Ms. K makes an appointment to return the next week.

In this session, the social worker has made a good start in helping the family with some of the psychological and social problems associated with Alzheimer's disease. Much work remains to be done. New problems will arise as the patients condition deteriorates and the family may call upon the social worker again for advice, guidance and counseling. Another family session may be needed when out-of-home placement becomes necessary. The social worker needs to remain alert to new problems and call them to the attention of the family to prevent crises. In addition, the social worker should help the family develop their independent functioning and problem-solving abilities. Only in this way will they be able to cope effectively with the responsibility of caring for their loved one.

A FINAL NOTE FOR COUNSELORS

To be successful, this counseling approach assumes a certain level of functioning on the part of family members. To the extent that true psychopathology exists within the family unit, family members will have difficulty working together effectively. In such cases, it may be possible for the social worker to identify one family member who copes better than others and work with that person to accomplish objectives. If this is not possible, the social worker's obligation is to protect the best interests of the patient. If abuse or neglect is suspected, this should be reported to appropriate investigative agencies without delay.

An alternative in problem cases is for one family member to apply for court conservatorship. This will begin a process in which the court investigates the various alternatives for care and makes an objective decision as to the most appropriate plan. If no family member is deemed capable of taking responsibility for the patient, an outside conservator may be appointed.

Caregivers who have no family support are especially vulnerable to the stress of caring for an Alzheimer's patient. Social workers need to be sensitive to symptoms of mental and physical breakdown which may signal an inability to adequately continue in the caregiving role. A thorough knowledge of mental disorders is necessary in order to recognize and treat such problems appropriately. In all cases, the social worker's primary objective should be to ensure patient and caregiver well-being through the use of appropriate clinical and social interventions.

REFERENCES

Family Survival Handbook: A Guide to the Legal, Financial and Social Problems of Brain Damaged Adults, Family Survival Project, San Francisco, 1981.

Gwyther, L. "Caring for Caregivers: A Statewide Family Support Program Mobilizes Mutual Self Help." Duke University Center for the Study of Aging and Human Development. (December 1982) Vol. 6, No. 4.

Lezak, M.D., Ph.D., "Living with the Characterologically Altered Brain Injured Patient," *Journal of Clinical Psychiatry,* 1978, Vol. 39, pp. 592-598.

Mace, N.L. and Rabins, P.V., M.D., *The 36-Hour Day,* The Johns Hopkins University Press, Baltimore, 1981.

Terry, R.D., M.D. and Katzman, R., M.D., "Senile Dementia of the Alzheimer Type," *Annals of Neurology,* November 1983, Vol. 14, No. 5, pp. 497-506.

Thomas, Lewis, M.D., Chancellor, Memorial Sloan-Kettering Cancer Center. Testimony presented at a joint hearing of the House Energy and Commerce Subcommittee and the House Aging Committee. August 3, 1983.

Alzheimer's Educational/Support Group: Considerations for Success— Awareness of Family Tasks, Pre-Planning, and Active Professional Facilitation

Sue Shibbal-Champagne, ACSW
D. M. Lipinska-Stachow, RN, BA

ABSTRACT. Alzheimer's Disease is a neurological disorder that causes memory and cognitive impairment. The progression of the disease causes distress to the afflicted person and the caregiver. The interactional patterns of family members are severely altered as the disease progresses. An Educational/Support group was formed to assist families in learning more about the disease, community resources, and effective coping strategies. In addition it was an opportunity to share emotional reactions and develop a network with others experiencing a common issue. The findings suggest that awareness of family tasks, pre-planning, time-limited sessions and professional facilitation were important elements in releasing the supportive potential of the group members and increasing their adaptive capacities.

INTRODUCTION

Presently there is no known cause or cure for Alzheimer's Disease in spite of continued research. The only means of direct intervention for the person afflicted is through symptomatic treatment of the behavioral and physical problems which occur as a result of the degenerative disease process. Deterioration of the person's condition results in a lessened awareness of self, the disease, members

Sue Shibbal-Champagne is a medical social worker at the Elliot Hospital, 995 Auburn Street, Manchester, NH 03103. D. M. Lipinska-Stachow is a consultant, educator, and counselor in the field of Alzheimer's Disease.

of the family, and relationships toward the outside world in general are severely altered. The family members and essentially the primary caregivers are constantly reminded of the changes taking place in their loved one. Their responses to the disease and how they cope with it will have an indirect effect on the person's behavior, and whether or not the person afflicted can continue to be cared for at home and within the community. Plans for alternative living, including a nursing home, may need to be discussed and explored.

During the early stages of the disease families may use denial to cope with the many changes taking place in the afflicted person, and the person with the disease may compensate for his/her losses by developing more elaborate memory cues. Families may unconsciously isolate the person or attempt to encourage his/her involvement in tasks beyond his/her capabilities. The caregiver may need to assume new responsibilities and tasks previously performed by the afflicted person (in an effort to reduce the incidence of a "catastrophic reaction" and exaggerated response to normal events). As the behavioral manifestations of the disease become more pronounced there is greater disruption in the family system, and regular social activities may become impossible. Friends and neighbors become detached and the spouse or caregiver also become isolated. Increasing demands may be placed upon adult children to contribute in many personal, financial, and emotional ways. Once in a position of parenting a parent, the adult child must relinquish the childhood illusion that one's parents are strong and independent.

These and many other complex interpersonal stressors combine to create upheaval, turmoil, frustration, sadness, and anger within the family system. Family members must begin to change their expectations of the person afflicted and begin to restructure their personal and physical environment. Families must be provided with an opportunity to express their feelings regarding caregiving responsibilities and changed expectations. They need encouragement to develop interests independently of the afflicted person and to acknowledge their loss and sadness as understandable response to irreversible change. In some instances the afflicted person's condition may require more than the caregiver can emotionally or physically provide unassisted. The provision of information regarding community resources and nursing home placement in an effort to facilitate a family decision for alternative care should be initiated at this time if not earlier.

These specific and frequently occurring issues as well as others · were the focus of our attention during the course of closed, time-limited groups with professional facilitation.

RATIONALE FOR THE GROUPS

Both authors had previous experience with open-ended groups for this population and found them to be unsuccessful in meeting the needs of the group members. It was felt that in the open-ended group modality dependency on the facilitators increased, it provided less opportunity for expression and self-direction, termination was ambiguous and no supportive network emerged. The findings of Steuer and Clark (1982) in their appraisal of open-ended vs. closed and structured support groups for this population indicated that their open-ended groups were unsuccessful with low participation and group disintegration, while closed, time-limited group were the most successful.

In developing the methodology for these groups, it was decided that the group should include some tasks, pre-planning, goal setting and time-limited closed sessions in order to release the supportive potential of the groups and to increase the member's adaptive capacities. The authors also agree with Borgman (1982) that, "Institutional support is a critical variable in the initiation process and that an established agency lends credibility and legitimacy to the process." Termination of the groups was incorporated into the group process from the initial meeting and therefore would not be an ending in itself but would provide a stepping stone that hopefully would enable the members to take their experiences from the formal group sessions and transfer them into their own life situations. In an effort to maintain a supportive link with the group members and to ascertain successful assimilation of newly acquired skills, a formal follow-up meeting was arranged for three months after the final session.

GROUP FORMATION

The groups were conducted in a 300 bed medical facility in a city of 90,000. The community is essentially middle class in socio-economic orientation with a high percentage of ethnic French Canadians and Greeks.

The age range of members was between 25 and 70. They were either retired or actively involved in a variety of employments. The afflicted relative of the group members was either living alone, with a group member or in a nursing home. Some members of the group were still raising children and others had adult children and grand-children.

It was felt that a more formal set of requirements facilitated group cohesion, attendance and participation. Specific group requirements were as follows:

1. The group shall only be open to family members or friends of a person with a diagnosis of Alzheimer's Disease (to rule out any confusion with reversible dementias).
2. Membership depends on a response to an advertisement in the local newpaper accepted in order until 12 spaces were filled.
3. Members agreed to attend all 8 sessions of 1 1/2 hours per week.
4. Members agreed to accept the confidentiality of the group.
5. Members may leave or enter the group at Session 2, after which no new members would be accepted for the remaining sessions.
6. There can be no substitution of a family member if a member is unable to attend a meeting and wishes to send another person in his/her place.
7. Members are required to complete (anonymously) a ''Burden Interview'' (Zarit et al., 1982) to determine the effects of the sessions on perceived levels of burden before and after the formal group sessions; and an evaluation of the organization and content of the group and facilitator performance.
8. A follow-up meeting will be scheduled for approximately three months from the last session.

GROUP DEVELOPMENT

The co-facilitators developed a working contract which clarified roles, mutual expectations, and objectives. Objectives for the groups became a semi-formal structure for the group sessions. The objectives for the group were as follows:

1. To establish an environment of mutual trust and caring which would involve the members in a natural desire to formulate a means of providing and receiving ongoing support following

the termination of the formal group sessions. (This was a covert objective and was not discussed with the group until after they had established the basis for their peer support group.)

2. To provide an educational/informational (cognitive) basis, which would increase the members' knowledge and understanding of the disease process and dispel some of the myths associated with aging, specifically with regard to Alzheimer's Disease.

3. To encourage an atmosphere of mutual trust and concern within which to explore and become aware of alternative methods of coping and to devise strategies for caregiving.

4. To maximize and increase members' awareness of strengths presently exhibited in the caregiving responsibilities.

5. To provide emotional/supportive (affective) basis conductive to open, confidential discussion allowing for honest sharing and communication of feelings.

ENGAGEMENT

Following an introduction of the co-facilitators and a description of their professional roles, the "Burden Interview" was administered to identify feelings of caregiver burden.

A working contract was established between group members and the facilitators. Members introduced themselves and gave a brief description of their situation and caregiving responsibilities. A lecture/discussion concerning diagnosis, characteristics and process of the disease was followed by the establishment of individual goals by each of the members.

During the next few sessions we continued to utilize inclusion methods as described by Schultz (1958) and provided unconditional positive regard to increase members' sense of belonging. Members were addressed by name, quiet members were drawn into discussion and each member was given the opportunity to speak or listen.

INTERACTION

A sense of cohesiveness developed quickly through mutual problem solving and common emotional responses. There was supportive group interchange as the members described their situations. Interaction increased between members and decreased between members and facilitators. There was also a shift from the general to the more specific areas of concern, and a greater willingness to share emotions, both negative and positive regarding caregiving responsibilities and relationships. Members who had placed a relative in a nursing home served as advisors for those who were considering institutional care. Members who had difficulty accepting their emotional responses to their relatives' behavior change received empathy and suggestions. We would agree with Yalom's contention (1970) that, "Early cohesiveness developing for early intermember identification facilitates a sense of trust." As common issues were discussed, honesty and receptiveness to ideas and suggestions were encouraged. The above developments were influenced by group dynamics and professional facilitation.

DISENGAGEMENT

During the final stages of the group our role as facilitators shifted to that of consultants as natural leadership developed among the members. The members used the final session to review, summarize, evaluate and plan for the future. They openly discussed how they had grown as individuals and as members of the group. The "Burden Interview" (Zarit, 1980) was readministered to consititute the post-test component of our evaluation of group effectiveness.

Prior to termination, group members spontaneously suggested establishing a telephone network for mutual exchange of ideas, support, and the planning of intermittent meetings in their homes. Group members volunteered to initiate the telephone network and to offer to have meetings in their homes.

The facilitators also planned a three month follow-up meeting at which time the informal network was functioning well and there was evidence that the members had maintained what they had gained from the formal group sessions.

DISCUSSION

The major (covert) goal of the facilitators was that the relationships which developed within the groups would be strong enough to generate the extension of those relationships beyond the formal sessions. This goal was repeatedly achieved. Further, the success of the groups was measured not only by the members' responses to written evaluation questions, but more importantly, by their per-cieved ability to cope more effectively, recognize and utilize ego strengths and reach out to each other.

These groups reflected unique components that were not utilized by other support groups of this nature which had been reviewed in the literature (Aronson, Levin, Lipkowitz, 1984; Gwyther, 1982; Hausman, 1979; LaVorgna, 1979; Stuer, Clark, 1982). The inclusion of the Burden Interview (Zarit, 1980) and a formalized follow-up presented tangible evidence of success in addition to the more subjective data mentioned above. These findings support Zarit's hypothesis that, "If burden has been assessed before an intervention, then administering the Burden Interview again after the intervention will indicate the degree of success of improvement" (Zarit, Orr, Zarit, 1983).

Pre-planned, task-oriented, time-limited sessions with professional facilitation were important elements in releasing the supportive potential of the groups and increasing the members' adaptive capacities. The findings of Hausman (1979), that the effectiveness of the groups . . . "prompts the recommendation that the short-term, time-limited, task-oriented format is appropriate . . . " lends credence to the above assertion.

CONCLUSION

It is felt that as a result of the pre-planned, task-oriented, and time-limited sessions, the group members were able to recognize and increase their adaptive capacity for coping and self-direction. The formation of the peer sharing network as a natural outgrowth of the formal group sessions, combined with a reduction in perceived levels of burden were strong indicators that growth beyond dependence and structure was easily transferable to the caregiver's own environment and that sharing had enabled them to decrease their own isolation.

REFERENCES

Aronson, M.K., Levin, G., & Lipkowitz, R. (1984). A community-based family/patient group program for Alzheimer's Disease. *The Gerontologist, 24,* 339-342.

Borman, L. 1982. Leadership in self-help/mutual aid groups. *Citizen Participation, 26.*

Gwyther, L.P. (1982). Caregiver self-help groups: Roles for the professional. *Generations,* 37-53.

48   SOCIAL WORK AND ALZHEIMER'S DISEASE

Hausman, C.P. (1979). Short-term counseling groups for people with elderly parents, *The Gerontologist*, 19, 102-107.

LaVorgna, D. (1979). Group treatment for wives of patients with Alzheimer's Disease. *Social Work in Health Care*, 5, 219-221.

Schulz, W.C. A three dimensional theory of interpersonal behavior. New York: Holt, Rhinehart, & Winston, 1958.

Steuer, J.L., Clark, E.O. (1982). Family support groups within a research project on dementia. *Clinical Gerontologist*, 1, 87-95.

Yalom, I.D. "Theory and Practice of Group Psychotherapy," Basic Books, New York, 1970, cited in Hausman, C.P.

Zarit, S.H., Reever, K.E., & Bach-Peterson, J. Relatives of the impaired elderly: Correlates of feelings of burden. *The Gerontologist*, 20, 649-654.

Zarit, S.H., Orr, N.K., & Zarit, J.M. Working with Families of Dementia Victim: A treatment manual. Andrus Older Adult Center UCLA/USC Long-Term Gerontology Center. U.S. Department of Health and Human Services, 1983.

Assisting Families in Coping With Alzheimer's Disease and Other Related Dementias With the Establishment of a Mutual Support Group

Margaret H. Simank, CSW, ACSW
Kenny J. Strickland, CSW, MSSW

PART I
DEFINITION

Alzheimer's disease, or dementia of the Alzheimer type, is the most common dementing illness. It affects 20-30 percent of the population who reach their mid-eighties, and it accounts for about half of the cases of dementia at any age. It was named after a German physician, Alios Alzheimer, who identified it in 1907 (Heston & White, 1983, p. 12). He identified a presenile form occurring in people as young as age 45, but it is actually the same disease as that found in the older population. Today, Alzheimer's disease is labeled Senile Dementia-Alzheimer's Type, generally abbreviated SDAT.

According to several studies cited by Wells (Teusink & Mahler, 1984, p. 152), Alzheimer's disease accounts for approximately 51 percent of dementia cases. More than three million Americans are affected to some degree by Alzheimer's disease, and more than one million, or 5 percent, of the elderly over age 64 are severely affected by it (Teusink & Mahler, 1984, p. 156). Today there is neither cure nor a treatment; a diagnosis of Alzheimer's disease carries with it a sentence of eventual mental emptiness. Although the progression of the disease is highly idiosyncratic—it may be 5 years

Margaret H. Simank and Kenny J. Strickland are affiliated with Kerrville State Hospital, PO Box 1468, Kerrville, TX 78028.

49

before it reaches the final stages, or 10 years, or 10 months, and there is no telling which faculties will be lost first and which maintained—the eventual result is complete disorientation and memory loss, and ultimately death (National Institutes of Health, 1980, p. 2).

According to Pajk, though the disease has been described, the cause is a mystery and the diagnosis is made virtually by the process of elimination. After all other disorders have been ruled out, a diagnosis of Alzheimer's disease is usually made on the basis of the type of symptoms and the way the symptoms progress over time. Confirmation, however, is only possible upon postmortem examination of brain tissue (Pajk, 1984, p. 217).

The behavioral hallmark of Alzheimer's disease seems to be memory loss, especially for recent events. But many other behavioral changes are caused by the illness. In its early stages, Alzheimer's disease can lead to inability to concentrate, anxiety, irritability, agitation, withdrawal, or petulance. Later the Alzheimer's patient may lose the ability to calculate, may exhibit lack of judgment, and may become disoriented as to time and place. (National Institutes of Health, 1980, p. 2). Some persons with Alzheimer's disease tend to wander about and lose their way; some become prone to temper tantrums; some are depressed; some forget the names of friends or family, or forget words or how to tell time. In the final stages of the disease, most Alzheimer's victims require assistance with all of the activities that encompass daily life and self-care, including urine and bowel control. It is a unique characteristic of Alzheimer's disease that the symptoms vary from patient to patient and sometimes from day to day in the same patient. It must be made clear in discussing this disease that no single symptom or behavior is completely predictable. However, the loss of recent memory seems to be universal (Powell & Courtice, 1983, p. 15).

PART II
THE IMPACT OF ALZHEIMER'S DISEASE ON A FAMILY

Alzheimer's disease is a family disease in the sense that the caregiver (spouse, child, or sibling usually) is involved in a progressively more active role as caregiver to a person who does not get better but who will require continuous physical care and increasing emotional support as they deteriorate both mentally and eventually, physically.

"Sadly they watch the slow disappearance of those characteristics that made up the unique personality of the afflicted loved one" (Powell & Courtice, 1983, p. 16-20). During this process of deterioration, called by some "the never ending funeral," caregivers experience the emotional trauma of a seemingly endless grief reaction to the loss of the person they knew and loved for so many years.

Various authors have described this grieving process around a framework similar to that developed by Elizabeth Kubler-Ross in her work, *On Death and Dying*, which consists of five stages: denial and isolation, anger, bargaining, depression, and acceptance (Powell & Courtice, 1983, p. 29; Teusink & Mahler, 1984, p. 156). *Alzheimer's Disease, a Guide for Families*, by Lenore Powell and Katie Courtice, published in 1983, provided us with a framework which closely follows that provided by Kubler-Ross to use in helping caregivers deal with the emotional trauma they experienced during the course of their relative's dementia.

Many families will often first notice memory problems in the patient but will choose to ignore these first early warning signs. Some memory loss is certainly common with the aging process, but when this loss exceeds mild forgetfulness, it is a sign of some kind of impairment in the brain. Some denial is certainly a normal part of coping with this disease, but many families carry this reaction to the extreme and fail to recognize grossly disturbed behavior (Teusink & Mahler, 1984, p. 33).

Anger develops as a result of the physical and emotional burdens placed on the caregiver, who very often has very little relief from the daily stresses of caring for their relative. The embarrassing behavioral problems presented by the dementia patient also increase the intensity of the angry feelings (Teusink & Mahler, 1984, p. 47).

At some point during the course of a relative's illness, many caregivers begin to feel useless and helpless. Subsequently, they may experience many of the classical symptoms of depression such as decreased physical vitality and a decrease in stamina (Teusink & Malher, 1984, p. 17).

As anger and depression decrease, guilt may become more prominent. Family members often feel guilty when they become angry at their relative's embarrassing behavior, even though they know this behavior is not a deliberate attempt to embarrass them. Intense guilt is also experienced when the caregiver makes the decision to place their relative in an alternate care facility.

Acceptance comes only after the relatives have understood both the disease process that is affecting the dementia patient, and they have found sufficient resources within themselves and the community to deal with the increased burden of care for the patient (Teusink & Mahler, 1984. p. 154).

Placing these emotional reactions in the context of a grieving process, we felt it would be helpful to many of our group members to integrate information about feelings and the process of grieving into our group format. This subsequently allowed group members an opportunity to work though this grief process within the group setting.

PART III
SUPPORT GROUP—PROCESS AND RESULTS

In the spring of 1983 our first mutual support/education and information group for family members (spouses, parents, children, etc.) of patients whose diagnoses included Alzheimer's disease or other related dementias was offered. The idea of offering this kind of group was to help relatives cope with the medical and emotional implications of their family members' illness through a sharing of experiences, ideas, information, and emotional support by group members with the aid of hospital social workers.

In the beginning a series of six weekly sessions or educational classes were held with a different aspect of the disease emphasized during each session. These sessions focused on such topics as: explanation of the dementias, implications of the disorder, problems in independent living and daily care, problems of behavior and mood, and family members' need for self-care and support. The first cycle of sessions were open only to those families with relatives in the Kerrville State Hospital with a diagnosis of Alzheimer's disease or any related dementia. In this early group, relatives certainly seemed anxious to learn, in some detail, information about Alzheimer's disease, its causes and possible treatment, and aspects of caring for the cognitively impaired relative. However, since this group of relatives had already hospitalized their loved one, issues emerged surrounding the devastating emotional impact of relinquishing the primary care giving role to our hospital staff.

It soon became evident to the authors that these relatives had undergone severe emotional and physical stress of some duration in caring for their demented loved ones, prior to seeking alternate care. The emotional conflicts created by the long term care of the patient in the home, other family and societal expectations to care. for one's own, and the stigma of seeking psychiatric hospital care, exacerbated the existing emotional pain of the loss of the unique personality of the loved one.

The primary needs, as expressed in the group discussions, were for information and an explanation of the disease process. It appeared to be especially important to have an opportunity to ventilate feelings and share experiences to alleviate the feelings of guilt, anger, loss, and isolation that were almost always felt by the caregiver. By isolation it is meant that feelings such as anger, embarrassment, depression, guilt, and grief were often commonly held by group members but had not been expressed due to fear of appearing rejecting of their afflicted loved one. A commonly held feeling expressed by several group members was the lack of understanding and empathy from other relatives, friends, neighbors, church, and community affiliations.

Another common theme that was expressed by these group members was a feeling that information about the disease process and subsequent behavior patterns of the dementia victim would have aided them in coping with the stresses of caring for their relative in the early stages of the illness. Reaching out to families in the community who were still caring for a dementia victim in their home became the focus for an ongoing support group which would offer both information and the support of those who could empathize with the normal series of emotional responses to caring for a victim of dementia.

Permission was sought and obtained to extend the group experience to family members in Kerrville and surrounding communities who were continuing to give care to a dementia patient in the home. The primary emphasis of these sessions was to educate the caregiver to alternative methods of coping with some of the difficulties encountered in caring for a memory impaired relative and to assist the relatives in increasing their awareness of these normal series of responses as the disease progressed.

Through the group process we allowed family members to work through the emotional reaction to the disease process. This reaction, as described earlier in this paper, consists of denial of the illness, anger as the reality of the disease becomes evident, depression as sorrow and loss are experienced, guilt over wishing for some respite from caring for the victim, and finally some acceptance or resolution as they work through the grief process and come to recognize that their relative is no longer the same person they knew and loved (Teusink & Mahler, 1984, p. 154).

Most relatives of Alzheimer's patients entering this group from the Kerrville community knew little or nothing about this common disease and were at a loss as to what to expect in the future concerning the course of the disease and the severe impact this disease has on the family. Some group members had relatives in the later stages, based mostly on the manifestation of an impaired memory for recent events. Those whose relatives were in the later stages of dementia (beginning to require total physical care, in addition to constant supervision) were often physically and emotionally exhausted and were struggling with the painful reality of alternate care placement. Several had tried nursing home placement and found this placement to be inadequate to meet the needs of their relative. The thought of mental hospital placement often carried a stigma which the family found difficult to accept. Association with family members who had already made a decision to seek commitment to the state hospital enables these relatives to more easily seek long-term mental hospitalization.

It has been the experience of many of the geriatric caseworkers at Kerrville State Hospital that in almost all instances of admission of severely demented patients, family members have gone to and sometimes exceeded their physical and emotional limits of coping with the perpetual task of caring for a severely demented patient. This was a task that they faced alone. Older spouses with children living away, or older siblings separated geographically from other extended family, were often totally responsible for providing care for the patient and eventually making the difficult decision to seek commitment. Physically and emotionally these people were often at risk themselves for incapacitation due to exhaustion and stress. Other group members who had previously placed their relatives at Kerrville State Hospital seemed particularly supportive and aware of the crisis facing those who were obviously no longer physically and emotionally able to care for their relative in the home. Of the six group members whose relatives were in the later stages of dementia and were being cared for in the home, four made the decision for alternate care placement during the group process. The two remaining group members seem to still be struggling with this decision.

Other group members whose relatives are in the early stages of dementia seem to be struggling with the day to day frustrations of caring for someone who is extremely forgetful and emotionally demanding, but who has not yet begun to manifest the more serious behavioral symptoms of advanced dementia. We observed in these two group members the issue of some denial, which is generally expressed by attempting to minimize the severity of the symptoms present. This may be an attempt to delay dealing with the impact of accepting a diagnosis with such a devastating prognosis. However, we feel that the step taken to seek more information about the long term impact of dementia, and the mutual support offered during the group experience, will enable these caregivers to seek continuing support of the group and provide them with access to available resources.

A monthly support group was established from interested members who had participated in the six-week information/education group. Many members had a desire to continue to meet in a less formal and less structured format primarily for the purpose of providing ongoing mutual support. Since the inception of the group, a monthly support group has been seen as the major long term support activity which will hopefully provide continued support for family members of hospitalized Alzheimer's victims, and also reach out into the community to offer information, education, and supportive services to relatives of dementia victims still in the home.

PART IV
IMPLICATIONS FOR SOCIAL WORKERS

Social workers working with the victims of a dementing illness are presented with a unique opportunity to intervene at what is usually a critical time for the family and the victim. The social worker must first be satisfied that a thorough diagnostic work up has been completed. Conditions that produce dementia resembling Alzheimer's disease include drug intoxication, depression, head injuries, brain tumors, and nutritional deficiencies such as pernicious anemia. Because many of these disorders may be reversed or cured with appropriate treatment, it is crucial that they be identified and all treatable causes of dementia ruled out through a thorough medical, neurological, and psychological assessment.

Social workers must first become aware of how devastating the effects of a dementing illness are both to the victim and the family. For the victim, referral to a conscientious and competent physician who is experienced in diagnostic procedures and can offer supportive treatment for dementia patients is the important first step. Family members have often been dealing with the problem behaviors of a dementia patient for some time before seeking professional help. Usually they are in a crises and may in fact be near their limits of coping. Intervention at this point consists of several steps. First of all, families want information. However, merely supplying printed information usually does not meet their needs. We have found that this quest for information is the beginning of a psychological process which requires some two-way communication not found in a pamphlet, and, unfortunately, not found often enough in a physician's office. Detailed information could be provided to educate these families about the dementias so that they will not develop unrealistic hopes that some new treatment will cure the dementias. Fad therapies are usually more harmful than beneficial. Improved therapies may be found in the future, but will be the result of careful and laborious research (Teusink & Mahler, 1984, p. 155).

Secondly, the caregiver must be given the opportunity to experience and express the normal series of emotional responses that were discussed earlier in this paper. Because families of patients with Alzheimer's and related dementias endure an ongoing grief process, they may need ongoing intervention and support to cope with the illness. These and other authors have shown that education and support can be effectively provided through relatives discussion and support groups (Powell & Courtice, 1983, p. 40; Teusink & Mahler, 1984. p. 155). Working with families in distress in a group is a traditional social work model using a traditional method to meet a need that will become more prevalent as our aged population grows.

Social workers must be secure in their abilities to deal with intense feelings of anger and depression and must have the ability to keep group members focused on the expression of these feelings. Distraction by topics that are not essential to working through the grief process must be redirected in order to allow expression of these often painful and uncomfortable feelings. What is important is to foster the process of working through the stages of denial, anger, depression, and guilt, so that some acceptance of the painful realities is achieved. Energy devoted to coping with these feelings can often be freed so that the caregivers can go on caring for the dementia patient at home or can make the very difficult and painful decision to place their loved one in an alternate care setting.

The initial series of group sessions were geared towards those family members whose relative was a victim of Alzheimer's disease or any other related dementia. However, in our efforts to contact relatives in the community still caring for a dementia victim in the home, several people were encountered who were curious about the disease and did not have a relative in the home. In addition, several health care professionals asked to attend the cycle of sessions for educational purposes only. The first community based group included one health care professional whose mother was a victim of Alzheimer's disease. Other health care professionals were put on a waiting list, as we had previously met the group quota with relatives of dementia victims. Group size was limited to an average of nine people in each session. This group was seen as successful for many of the relatives who attended since the focus and cohesiveness of the group allowed the group members to share feelings and to receive support from each other.

For a variety of reasons the second community based group was much larger, with an average of 14 members per session. This group was a mixture of health care professionals, interested persons from the community, and a small number of relatives of dementia patients. The group process which allowed relatives to express mutual feelings observed in the previous group, was for the most part absent in this particular group. Because of the large size of this group and the fact that most of the group members had not experienced the emotional trauma of caring for a demented relative, the intensity and willingness to share the many feelings was not present. The focus on feelings and the cohesiveness of the group experience, based on mutual loss, gave way instead, to a broad lecture, question and answer format, and diluted the intensity of the effort of working through the normal series of responses described earlier in this paper. Therefore, in the future, group membership will be limited to relatives of dementia patients.

There certainly exists a need for health care professionals to learn more about how Alzheimer's disease impacts on a family and about how awareness of "Alzheimer's disease as a family disease" can enable them to work more supportively and effectively with both the dementia patient and the family members. A workshop of 3-4 hours duration is being planned for presentation to health care professionals working with dementia patients and their families.

Detailed information, referrals to existing resources, and a detailed explanation of the disease process in laymen's terms seem to be the most appropriate type of presentation to be made to community groups. Community education appears to be vital in the early detection of Alzheimer's disease. Until the general public is aware of the early stages of the disease and has an idea of what to look for in the disease process, intervention will most likely be made during the later stages of the disease process, making the emotional trauma much more intense for those forced to cope with it.

Social workers employed in settings where families suffering the ordeal of caring for a dementia victim are referred, can help ease the emotional impact of the disease upon the family by helping them learn how the disease process impacts upon them emotionally. While we have been able to devote the time and energy to this group experience on a regular basis over the last 18 months, there is an awareness that our positions in such a facility where many dementia patients are hospitalized is somewhat unique. The real need for this type of group experience lies in the community where families do not have access to the resources that are available in our hospital. As our population ages and dementia becomes more of a focused problem, the need for supportive community based groups will increase. Mutual support groups led by social workers offer relatives information, referral to existing resources in the community, and most important, a setting where they can feel acceptance, can share the enormous emotional burden, and can receive support and empathy from those who have experienced the same kind of grief and loss.

REFERENCES

Heston, Leonard L., MD; White, June A. *Dementia: A Practical Guide to Alzheimer's Disease and Related Illnesses.* W.H. Freeman and Company, New York, NY and San Francisco, CA, 1983.

Mace, Nancy L.; Rabins, Peter V., MD. *The 36-Hour Day: A Family Guide to Caring for Persons with Alzheimer's Disease, Related Dementing Illnesses, and Memory Loss in Later Life.* The Johns Hopkins University Press, Baltimore, MD 1981.

National Institute of Health *Alzheimer's Disease, A Scientific Guide for Health Practitioners,* November 1980, (NIH Publication No. 81-2251) Washington, DC, U.S. Government Printing Office.

Pajk, Marilyn, RN, MS. Alzheimer's Disease, Inpatient Care. *The American Journal of Nursing,* February 1984, Volume 84, No. 2. pp. 216-222.

Powell, Lenore S., Ed. D.; Courtice, Katie. *Alzheimer's Disease: A Guide for Families.* Addison-Wesley Publishing Company, Reading, MA, 1983.

Reisberg, Barry, MD. *A Guide to Alzheimer's Disease.* The Free Press, New York, 1981.

Teusink, J. Paul, MD; Mahler, Susan, MSW, ACSW. Helping Families Cope with Alzheimer's Disease. *Hospital and Community Psychiatry,* February 1984, Volume 35, No. 2, pp. 152-156

Adult Day Care:
An Integrated Model

Patricia M. Kirwin, MEd

ABSTRACT. For frail elders and those afflicted with Alzheimer's Disease, adult day care is a maturing service option linking clients and their caregivers with formal community supports. Integrating two programs for the aging, such as an adult day care program and a senior center, increases participant service options while decreasing service cost.

Based on the results of a state-funded demonstration integrating an adult day care program into a senior center, there is significant evidence that adult day care programs afford participants and their caregivers an opportunity to achieve more satisfactory lives than they were formerly leading. From experience, we know that for a few, a miracle seems to happen. For others, progress is measurable even though their capacity for independent living may still be limited. Whoever the person, or for whatever reason it is needed, adult day care provides the link to services that maintain or improve the client's health status (Blaser, 1983). For the client with Alzheimer's disease, these benefits are enhanced by providing caregivers linkage with community services. These include access to family support groups, respite care, and an array of in-home services.

Within the last ten years, adult day care has emerged as a long-term care alternative to increase the options available to the impaired elderly and thereby improve their quality of life (O'Brien,

Patricia M. Kirwin, 634 Knox Road, Wayne, PA 19087, was a graduate intern at COSA during the period of this demonstration. She was a student at the Bryn Mawr College Graduate School of Social Work and Social Research.

This demonstration was funded by the Pennsylvania Department of Aging, Deleware County Services for the Aging (COSA) and Leisure Services of Upper Darby Township, Deleware County, PA during the 1983 fiscal year. The annotated bibliography following this article was presented at a paper session on Adult Day Care at the Annual Meeting of the Northeastern Gerontological Society, Philadelphia, PA, April 1984.

1982). The Menorah Home and Hospital for the Aged in Brooklyn, New York founded the first day care in 1957 (Butler & Lewis, 1982). In 1974, the federal government provided support for a state-of-the-art paper on adult day care. There were fewer than fifteen locations from which programs could be selected for study (Robins, 1981). Today, there are more than 900 such programs.

The utilization of knowledge gained from ten to fifteen years' experience with therapeutic and medical model day care programs and the increasing need for alternatives for long-term care has only recently generated the concept of a social model for adult day care. There is, therefore, a scarcity of research findings on this segment of the continuum of service for the aging.

Implementing an adult day care program in an existing facility, such as a senior center, has the benefit of an overall reduction of program cost including the sharing of professional staff. Aside from cost, adult day care programs located within senior centers enhance social interaction between the well and the frail elderly (PA Dept. of Aging, 1983). While adult day care clients do not require a full-time nurse or aide at home, they generally need a level of supervision not easily delivered by informal care providers in residential or current senior center settings. The core services of adult day care programs include the provision of meals and social activities in a protective setting. This demonstration program also includes nursing supervision, linkage to community social services, health facilities and transportation. Individual care plans are developed for each participant which are periodically reviewed and updated in accordance with individual needs (Adult Day Care Programs, 1982).

Through Delaware County Services for the Aging (COSA), an area agency, service managers reassess all clients every 4-6 months and with the client and/or the caregiver establish a care plan which includes the needed client services from the continuum of services available through the aging network. The initial assessment, reassessment, and care-plan are integral to the Service Management System of the county network. As a decentralized, co-ordinated approach to meeting client needs, service managers are professional social workers located in community senior centers and, therefore, readily available to clients and well acquainted with appropriate neighborhood resources to meet their clients' needs.

Recently, at a state conference on adult day care, Betty (Shepherd) Ransom, Program Coordinator, National Institute on Adult Day Care, stated in her keynote address the pressing need for this service in supporting the physically and/or mentally impaired and the incontinent. As with nursing homes, only a small percent of the population will ever utilize an adult day care program. But, as the aging population continues to swell—the largest growth segment of the population is among those over 75—the number of participants that percentage represents indicates that the service will continue to expand and professionally develop to meet a community need in fulfilling the desire of impaired elders to remain in the community supported by formal and informal services. In response to their increased awareness of the additional number of impaired elders, including those with Alzheimer's disease and in order to contain institutional costs, state and federal governments support this service. While the percent of the population with this disease is not increasing, there are higher numbers of victims due to the increased number of aging individuals in the general population. There is a need for program models and the sharing of program results.

SERVICE INTEGRATION

A senior center was chosen for the implementation of an adult day care program based on the premise that in serving the elderly:

1. Services are most accessible at the community level (PA Dept. of Aging, 1983).
2. Senior centers, when properly staffed, are the most appropriate service delivery focal points because a relationship of trust and respect has clearly been established through the delivery of necessary and tangible services.
3. Optimal community living by the impaired, frail elder can be achieved only if special service options are available (Gottesman, 1975).
4. Families and caregivers desire to and will provide primary care for the impaired, frail elder if given special support such as a day care program offers (Blaser, 1983).
5. There exists in the community untapped resources which can be captured to improve the lives of the elderly.
6. Older people can and want to contribute their resources to the community (*Aging,* 1983; Gurewitsch, 1982; Hochschild, 1973; Zaki & Zaki, 1982).
7. Center programming, adjusted to include the frail elder, can only be considered successful if the regular center participants

accept modifications without feelings of alienation or loss (*Aging*, 1983).

However, a word of caution should be included. The population served is old, and will be getting older. Although we may grieve for an older person we have known who must be admitted to a hospital or nursing home, or who dies, we place an undue burden on the program if each admission or death is considered a failure (Padula, 1974). We do not set ourselves up to reverse the aging process. In *Death and Dying*, Dr. Kübler-Ross, who has worked so sensitively with dying patients, emphasizes that she is not helping people to die but helping them to live until they die. A day care program for the aged has the same purpose—to help people live as fully as is possible for as long as is possible.

FAMILIES AND INDIVIDUALS WHO MOST BENEFIT FROM ADULT DAY CARE

Those who benefit most from this service include:

1. *Families and Caregivers* by providing respite from the continuous pressures of full-time care, a vital release of significant family value—perhaps allowing for employment (Blaser, 1983).
2. *Frail Elders* who need social contact in a highly supervised setting.
3. *Current Senior Center Members* who have become more dependent, requiring more individual attention than is possible in the senior center.
4. *The Well Spouse* who is not able to leave the frail mate unattended in order to participate in senior center activities. When attending the center with a day care program, the couple experiences peer involvement, thus reducing the isolation of both.

SERVICE DESCRIPTIONS OF AN ADULT DAY CARE PROGRAM

In response to the concerns and assessed needs of program participants the following are seen as basic program services:

1. *Socialization.* A fundamental belief of this demonstration has been that individual needs should be met at the community level. One basic need is for socialization. Through program integration, we believe this has happened. Through study of other integrated day care models, we believed socialization techniques would emerge from the participants themselves as empathy and caring developed between people (*Aging*, 1983). In fact, this is what happened. The move from passive to active program acceptance emerged as senior center participants' empathic and caring feelings were individually expressed.
2. *Health Service.* The program director, a registered nurse, supervises medication, leads discussions on health issues, monitors health functioning on a daily basis, and helps caregivers clarify health-related concerns while integrating the client with the health services and providers as needed.
3. *Nutrition.* Nutrition counseling and informal education are integral to the small discussion groups for the day care members who also participate in center nutrition education activities including quarterly presentations by the county hospital.
4. *Transportation.* While a few family members were able to provide transportation, it was assumed, for planning purposes, that all clients would need round-trip transportation. A county transportation consortium, eligible for state reimbursement through lottery funds, expanded its regular senior center services to accommodate these clients. Transportation was integrated with regular center transportation whenever it was possible to accommodate the day care client's schedule.
5. *Family Support Groups.* Supplemental to the real help provided to caregivers through the availability of the day care program, staff assists families by informing them of other support and respite options.
6. *Staff Needs and Training.* The competency of the staff is of utmost importance in the effective operation of the program (O'Brien, 1982). While *Standards for Adult Day Care* prepared by the National Institute on Day Care, a constituent unit of the National Council on the Aging (March, 1984), specifies one staff participant for each eight participants, a review of the literature, discussion with experienced day care program administrators, and our own experience, indicate that a more responsive ratio is one-to-five (Rose Locker, Retired Director, Day Care Program, Philadelphia Geriatric Center;

Eunice James, Waxter Senior Center, Day Care Program, Baltimore).

INTEGRATION DILEMMAS

The issue of whether these two services and populations could be integrated in a meaningful and efficient manner was crucial for senior center and day care services in the county.

As focal points for service entry and delivery, the well established senior center network population is aging and therefore an increasing emphasis on serving the older, more frail participant has become needed.

Dilemmas confronting the goal of integration were many:

1. If the center is an ideal focal point because of its acceptability to the traditionally non-service using well-elderly population, how would we maintain that image when focusing more services on the frail-elderly?
2. How accepting would seniors be of those they viewed as requiring more of the limited resources available to "their center"?
3. How might a program prevent members from feeling a loss of control and ownership over yet another area of their lives?
4. Would the senior center community accept the image of the center as a service provider as well as a site for recreational activities?
5. Would center members accept and welcome the frail, the advanced Alzheimer's victim, the wheel-chair bound inarticulate client, and the inherent service modifications into their facility?

MAJOR FINDINGS

Major findings of this demonstration indicate the value of service integration to the maintenance and supported independence of frail clients. The integration of two services for the aging such as a senior center and an adult day care program allows for a back-and-forth flow of participants as their needs and abilities allow. As previous research has indicated, transportation continues to be the vital link between isolation at home and socialization and access to services available through senior centers.

The benefits of a pleasant, positive, consistent manner, exercised at all times by program staff is beyond our ability to quantify or qualify. These qualities were also stressed by Betty (Shepherd) Ransom, in her above referenced keynote address, as critical for program success. Without a doubt, the presence or absence of these qualities will influence the outcome of other attempted programs.

The role of caregiver support is also vital in maintaining the frail within the community. Therefore, advising families of the range of services available to assist them in their caregiving role is essential. An adult day care program located within a senior center allows for formal and informal advisement through the director (a nurse) and through service managers and client service directors (social workers).

Caregivers appear to benefit from groups where they may build support, share problems and coping strategies, and become connected to services to help them provide a level of sustaining care. *Clients also revealed a need for individual or group opportunities to express their feeling and to extend their coping strategies with their growing dependence.*

While Alzheimer's disease is now the fourth major disease of the aged, among this program's 35 unduplicated participants, it ranked first with 13 of the participants having Alzheimer's disease; 9 arthritis; 8 stroke paresis; 5 diabetes; and 4 cardiac problems. All clients have at least one impairment. Fourteen of the 35 have 2 impairments. One client has 3 impairments. For 17 of the 35 participants, their spouse is their primary caregiver. Several of these caregiving spouses attend the senior center.

Concern for the integration dilemmas in this project proved to be the anxiety of program managers rather than of participants. Interest in expanding center services to include day care had been long-standing with several members including the Vice-President of the Senior Center Board who voiced her desire to see expanded center services capable of including her older, frail brother for whom she was caring.

Prior to becoming a demonstration site, four open forums to discuss the anticipated day care integration and to exchange questions and answers were held with regular senior center participants. After the acceptance of the proposed demonstration, the operational plan was reviewed step-by-step with an interested group of center participants. Two members who actively and positively anticipated the coming integrated service and who were recognized as leaders, spoke informally to center members who were more passive. While information was continuously, informally circulated, few questions were actually asked. The attitude seemed to be one of wait-and-see.

One week prior to the official opening, the day care director spoke in an especially reassuring manner with regular center participants to inform them of the arrival of the program (finally!) and attempted to allay any unspoken or silent fears that may have been present. Assurances were given that adult day care was just one link in the care continuum. Support of regular center members for the new day care participants was encouraged. Several center women knitted lap robes for the anticipated attendees (PA Aging Information Memorandum #83-33, p.4). Two months into the program, the director again spoke with senior center participants to inform them of how the program was going from staff's point-of-view and to invite their thoughts and concerns. There appeared to be agreement on the success of the program integration to date.

In an already receptive environment as was present at this center, "problems" of integration came to be viewed as welcome challenges. We believed that these challenges would be met through solutions that would come from the regular senior center members themselves (*Aging,* 1983; Zaki & Zaki, 1982). This, in fact, did occur. Sharing meals, celebrations, and recreational activities fostered caring, supportive relationships. The most physically impaired day care client remained capable of sharing, giving, and receiving in the emerging relationships.

Of all the integrated activities, music seemed to more deeply affect the larger number. For the most part, initial attempts at integrating activities met with passive acceptance. As the program began to reveal its potential and center participants began to interact on their own terms, more active acceptance developed and eventually matured.

ADVOCACY NEEDS

Because we tend to become intimately involved with the aging segment of the society as part of our profession, succumbing to inertia in our mission of advocacy is a daily danger. We may come to believe that society is experiencing a reduction in ageism, but as with racism and sexism, the need to advocate for non-discrimination between the generations conceivably will never end. Even those we serve try to deny the natural maturing process. Surviving the years is not seen as an achievement but rather as a stigma! There is an immediate alive need for Area Agencies, State Agencies, and National Associations to become advocates of the services they are designed to provide through the use of public relations and marketing strategies. With adult day care, it is imperative for communities, that is, each of us, to recognize the needs of frail elders and their families, and either to accept the day care approach currently being offered or to suggest alternative services to meet the recognized need. Families, with all their loving strength, cannot meet their obligations for the care of frail elders without either the support of the community or becoming victims themselves. Adult day care is just such a community support fully capable of linking frail elders, those afflicted with Alzheimer's disease, and their caregivers with formal and informal community services. Integrating two aging programs, such as an adult day care program and a senior center, increases participant service options while decreasing costs in the continuum of community care.

AFTER NOTE

The success of this demonstration program has led to the County Area Agency on Aging's full funding of this program and the planned funding for an additional four to six adult day care programs within the next fiscal year.

DAY CARE BIBLIOGRAPHY
ANNOTATED

Adult Day Programs for the Elderly Proceedings. Published with the cooperation of the Publications and Advertising Office, Utica College of Syracuse University, January, 1982.

Reports from a Symposium on Day Care Programs for the Elderly intended to broaden the range of view of those who guide and deliver community-based services. The results of the three day effort cover all facets of the current status of this service delivery.

Adult Daycare Services: An Introduction to the Literature, Selected Topics in Long-Term Care. Vol. 2. By ELM Services, Inc. for the Administration on Aging. Washington, D. C.: Sept. 1980.

Examines several Adult Day Care medical models but concludes that at this juncture there is no way to evaluate whether any of the various approaches are "better" or "best." Except for descriptions of programs, the entire adult/geriatric day care literature is one large gap. "Policies & purposes & programs have been described, but virtually no evaluation has been accomplished."

Blaser, Peg R., "Illinois Adult Day Care Parallels National Trend." *Perspective on Aging,* XII, No. 3, May/June, 1983, pp. 20-23.

Illinois' Day Care pattern reveals that the clients are generally more mobile than persons receiving in-home services. Respite from the continuous pressures of full time care provides a vital release that can be of significant family value.

Butler, Robert N., M. D. and Myrna I. Lewis, *Aging & Mental Health.* St. Louis: The C. V. Mosby Co., 1982.

"Day Care Center Brings New Perspective to Mt. Vernon Elderly." *Aging,* No. 337, Mar./Apr. 1983, pp. 32-33.

The nearest present example of true integration. The issue of how regular members and frail clients become integrated is described: regular members in their own time and in their own way accept and develop empathy for more dependent members.

"Day Care Center Delivers Several Types of Services." *Aging,* Nos. 277-278, Nov./Dec. 1977, pp. 26-27.

In Arlington County, Virginia, the Madison Center, a Day Care facility opened in 1976—a coordinated approach to social services delivery and a professional and financial pooling of resources. The intent is to rehabilitate those who have been hospitalized for mental problems, to keep older people functioning, and to prevent further deterioration and possible institutionalization.

Gottesman, Leonard E., David Eisenberg and Barbara Ishizaki, *Day Care Services for Old Disabled People.* Phila.: Philadelphia Geriatric Center, 1975.

Gurewitsch, Eleanor. "Geriatric Day Care. The Options Reconsidered." *Aging,* Nos. 329-330, July/August, 1982, pp. 21-26.

> While this represents a medical model, lunch is an integrated activity with a Senior Center program housed under the same roof.

Gustafson, Elizabeth. "Day Care for the Elderly." *The Gerontologist,* February 1974, pp. 46-49.

> Author favors the medical model but regards the social model as "primarily a social program for the frail, moderately handicapped, or slightly confused older person who needs care during the day for some part of the week either because he lives alone and cannot manage on his own, or because his family needs relief at times in order to keep him at home."

Hochschild, Arlie Russell. *The Unexpected Community.* Berkeley: University of California Press, 1973.

> Participant observation report of the aged in lower-class apartment housing before the advent of Area Agencies on Aging. Research demonstrates empathic helping nature of relationships among cohorts.

Koenen, Robert E. "Adult Day Care, A Northwest Perspective." *Journal of Gerontological Nursing,* 6, No. 4 (1980), pp. 218-221.

> Day Care centers seek to intervene sooner and at less cost in order to maintain the individual at the highest level of independence. Respite for care-givers is a secondary goal of this service.

Leary, Florence. "Overcoming a Client's Resistance to Day Care." *National Institute on Adult Daycare News,* 2, No. 3 (1982), pp. 3-4.

> It is important to build a relationship of trust, to reduce anxiety about the Center, and to make Adult Day Care a non-threatening option.

Lorenze, Edward J., et al. "The Geriatric Day Hospital." Report presented at the 26th Annual Meeting of the Gerontological Society, Miami Beach. 7 Nov., 1973.

" . . . day centers should be completely non-institutionalized and be offered in a neighborhood house, thus assuring a "homey" environment.

Meltzer, Judith W. "Respite Care: An Emerging Family Support Service." Centers for the Study of Social Policy: Washington D. C.: Administration on Aging. National Conference on Social Welfare. June, 1982.

This paper assesses the current state of knowledge about respite care services which offer relief to spouses or relatives caring for a dependent or disabled person.

O'Brien, Carole Lium. *Adult Day Care, A Practical Guide.* California: Wadsworth Health Services, 1982.

While a medical model classic, social models can utilize much of this "how-to."

O'Brien, Carole Lium, "Exploring Geriatric Day Care: An Alternative to Institutionalization," *Journal of Gerontological Nursing,* 3, No. 5, September, October, 1977, pp. 26-28.

A psychological model is one in which there is a small proportion of professionals to participants—less emphasis on health services, more emphasis on social services and participants who suffer from isolation, depression, and loneliness. O'Brien recommends further research into tangible and intangible outcomes by cost effectiveness and cost benefit analysis.

Ohnsorg, Dorothy W. "The Role of Therapy in Adult Day Care." *National Institute of Adult Day Care News,* 3, No. 2, Spring, 1983.

Indicates the importance of the recreational therapist in any Adult Day Care Program.

Padula, Helen. *Developing Day Care for Older People.* Technical Assistance Monograph prepared for the Office of Economic Opportunity by the National Council on the Aging, September 1972, reprinted 1974.

PA Department of Aging. "Adult Day Care." Aging Information Memorandum #83-33, October 17, 1983.

The Memorandum is a clear indication of the Department's intent to stimulate the birth of social model ADC programs in order to evaluate their client success and their cost.

Robins, Edith. "Adult Day Care: Growing Fast But Still for Lucky Few." *Generations,* Spring, 1981, pp. 22-23.

Article traces brief Day Care history, funding sources (for medical models) and lists 12 Adult Day Care programs of the medical variety.

Stabler, N. "The Use of Groups in Day Centers for Older Adults." *Social Work with Groups,* 4, No. 3-4, 1981, pp. 49-58.

Examples are provided of a number of group interactions as evidence of the effectiveness of group treatment for older isolated people.

Trupiano, Florence, Mc. *Initial Planning Considerations for Developing an Adult Day Care Center.* North Texas State University: Center for Studies in Aging, May, 1978.

Along with planning data this book contains a now dated but nevertheless excellent review of the literature.

Wood, Suzanne and William P. Harris. "Adult Day Care, A New Modality." *The Journal of Long Term Care Administration,* IV, Spring, 1976, p. 19.

Provides definitions and directions for this service.

Zaki, Gamal and Sylvia Zaki. *Day Care As a Long-Term Care Service.* Brown University: Rhode Island College Gerontology Center, 15 February, 1982.

Compares 10 ADC centers. Zaki, in looking at the Levindale Adult Day Treatment Center in Baltimore, found a psychosocial model to be superior to a health model: "Day Care participants became a social group. They interacted with each other and planned for themselves." This is a family service. It's important to involve the family.

The Milieu Standard
for Care of Dementia
in a Nursing Home

Helene D. Grossman, MS
Audrey S. Weiner, MPH
Michael J. Salamon, PhD
Nelson Burros, CSW

ABSTRACT. Recent attention has been directed toward providing
specialized skilled nursing facility care for patients suffering from
dementia. This paper explores and details how The Hebrew Home
for the Aged at Riverdale developed such a unit and its applicability
for the provision of appropriate care to demented elderly in other
settings. The leadership roles of professional care staff, particularly
the social worker in the development of this project are highlighted.

We know that the pain and misery which is the fate of thou-
sands of the mentally impaired aged among us can be avoided
or ameliorated. What is required is humane, compassionate
care in a milieu which does not impose excess demands but
rather supports and nurtures. This should be our task and our
goal. (Goldfarb, 1973)

INTRODUCTION

If we view the past fifteen years as the era of popularization,
destigmatization and scientific discovery of the various diseases of
dementia, then consideration can and should now be devoted to the

Helene D. Grossman is Associate Executive Director, Audrey S. Weiner is Assistant Administrator, Michael J. Salamon is Director, Research Division, and Nelson Burros is Director of Social Services at The Hebrew Home for the Aged at Riverdale, 5901 Palisade
Avenue, Riverdale, NY 10471.

73

still present issues of management of patients with severe cognitive disorders within institutional long-term care settings.

In the past decade, the long-term institutionalized geriatric patient who presented behavioral management problems, whether functional or organic, was referred to the staff social worker for a reactive resolution. "Progressive facilities, may have further responded by psychiatric or psychological evaluation, including various elements of differential diagnosis. Inevitably, the patient was viewed and labelled as a "problem"—to other patient care staff and patients.

Silverstone and Weiss (1983) have suggested that the challenge of the social work profession is heightened by changes which inevitably occur within long-term care . . . "goals are defined by the problem and the needs of the frail impaired client, wherever he is encountered along the continuum." These authors have suggested that such a continuum extends to and within a progressive patient placement system in institutional long-term care settings.

This paper describes the process and outcome of a one-year study at The Hebrew Home for the Aged at Riverdale (HHAR) a 951 bed long-term care facility in the Bronx, New York which led to the development of a special care unit (SCU) for the moderately to severely demented patient. The background for the development of the SCU for individuals with similar behavioral problems whether of a functional, or organic nature, including the instrumental role taken by the Social Services Department throughout the amalgam of institutional and interdepartment processes will be detailed. Also explored is the replicability of the program within other long-term institutional settings.

Similar to most other voluntary, non-profit, long-term care institutions, HHAR has, over its seven-decade history, evolved and developed in response to changing political, economic, social and demographic trends. In 1913, the Home began as a small neighborhood shelter for 37 homeless adults. The facility grew in size and scope of programs and services as a response to the growing numbers and needs of the aged population; the birth of the nuclear family, the inception of Medicare and Medicaid programs, and; advances in the fields of gerontology and geriatrics. The development in more recent years of an increasing number of community-based programs (Koff, 1982), combined with the shrinking of the institutional mental health system (Borus, 1981; Stotsky, 1970; Zimmer et al., 1984) more rigorous criteria for admission to long-term care institutions (Curtis & Bartlett, 1984) and an explosive demographic increase in the 75+ and 85+ age cohort, has weighted the applicant pool to long-term care institutions toward those with significant physical and/or psycho-social dysfunctions and needs. Similarly, the consequence of survivorship have created a current resident pool who, as a result of gradual physical and mental deterioration, also have heightened needs.

In 1983, HHAR had six ICF/HRF living areas and ten skilled nursing (SNF) units. Included within these SNF units were two ''intensive units'' developed 25 years ago, as ''infirmary units'' for patients identified as management concerns, and/or those acutely ill patients requiring very substantial nursing care. The primary difference between these and the other SNF units was the higher level of nursing staffing. In more recent years these units were used only for the difficult to manage patients. A long waiting list for transfer and admission to these units as well as the expressed concern of alert patients and institutional staff about the patient mix on the other eight SNF units prompted an evaluation of the current patient profile and institutional need. Also included in the evaluation was an assessment of the current purpose and adequacy of existing ''intensive units.''

THE LITERATURE

Considerable controversy has been generated over the appropriateness of segregating patients in long-term care settings according to their level of need. These arguments are not dissimilar from the related discussions regarding segregation of the aged from other age groups for social interactions (Tobin, Davidson, & Sack, 1976). The arguments favoring age-integrated interactions suggest that the aged generally prefer to be with other age groups. It gives them a sense of purpose, allows them to develop a sense of leadership and provides for a broad range of socialization (Daum, 1982). Those advocating age-segregated activities suggest, however, that older adults, faced with many losses associated with their status and condition turn to each other for support. Older adults according to this position are more favorably disposed to one another, and identify more with one another than with other age groups (Rosow, 1974).

A similar debate extends to long-term care, offering again no conclusive evidence (Ablowitz, 1983). It has been suggested that patients with varying levels of clinical need should be integrated on the same unit, i.e., "mainstreaming." It is postulated that integration will result in a beneficial impact for all patients on the integrated unit. Those with lower levels of need may enjoy and benefit from helping the more impaired patients. Those patients who are more impaired may benefit from the companionship of a patient who functions at a healthier level.

In contrast, Bowker (1982) reported that a great deal of evidence indicates that mixing of patients with different levels of functioning may result in a strong sense of dehumanization. Specifically, integration of patients may cause the healthier patients to avoid the more impaired ones for fear of becoming as ill as they are. This could, in turn, contribute to reciprocal feelings of isolation and depression (Butler & Lewis, 1982; Ablowitz, 1983). Furthermore, the severely impaired patients response to a "typical" skilled nursing unit may be explosive or result in a withdrawal from a setting which is too demanding. In contrast, an oriented, rational individual may find the supportive, environmentally modified unit confining, too circumscribed and devoid of interest (Goldfarb, 1973). Concerns also exist regarding the need for additional training and ongoing support of staff assigned to special units to preclude burnout, staff turnover and related costs (Pavur & Smith, 1983).

While this debate may require an additional decade to resolve, a number of long-term care institutions, sensing the urgency for provision of special care, have designed or are currently developing "special care units" for patients with significant cognitive impairment or behavioral problems due to dementia or related disorders.

APPLICATION OF THE THEORETICAL

The question of homogeneous versus heterogeneous placement by patient function and clinical need is not simply a question of greater preference on the part of patients or staff but also relates to the staff's ability to better address patient need. To determine the staff's feelings to both of these issues a survey was performed on the 10 skilled nursing units at HHAR in 1983 (Salamon, 1983). Forty percent of the clinical care staff, including social workers, doctors, nurses, aides and physical and occupational therapists were randomly selected and asked to respond to a questionnaire. Two major issues were addressed by the questionnaire;

A. Could better care be provided to the patients if the units were segregated by behavior and function?

B. Would the patients be more comfortable if they were so segregated?

Results of that survey can be seen in Table 1. Overall, 76% of the clinical care staff felt that they could perform a better job in providing more direct service if the units were segregated. Eighty-three percent of the clinical care staff felt that patients would feel more comfortable if they were segregated by level of care. While not statistically significant in comparison to other patient

Table 1

SNF Unit	Better Care Could Be Provided	Patients Would Be More Comfortable
1	64%	88%
2	86%	100%
3	83%	67%
4	60%	60%
5	60%	80%
6	75%	75%
7	60%	80%
8	60%	80%
9	83%	80%
10	100%	100%
Overall	76%	83%

Table 1: Staff responses to questions regarding ability to provide better care if specialized units were segregated and feelings of patients being more comfortable.

care providers nursing and medical staff were most supportive of a homogeneous approach to patient placement. This may have been influenced by their experience with such special units as cardiac and intensive care units during their training as well as their orientation to efficiency and effectiveness. The social work staff, was initially less enthusiastic of segregating patients by need. They were perhaps influenced by the notion that "the stronger patients could positively help and impact the less oriented patients"; and the social workers' concern regarding possible stigmatization of individuals and groups.

This survey was initially prompted by administrative concerns regarding the impact upon the facility of the increased numbers of patients with dementing illnesses and how to best provide care for the individual patient, as well as the total population. These issues were simultaneously expressed by HHAR's Resident Council. Given the facility's belief in the importance of the role of the Resident Council in decision making that effects their lives and encouragement to bring institutional concerns into the open (Getzel, 1983), the Director of Social Services, the designated staff person, arranged a forum for discussion of the issues. The Council voiced their concern that patients who were most alert and oriented were increasingly more uncomfortable when increased numbers of less alert patients, some with disruptive or antisocial behaviors were placed on the same unit. Poignantly expressed was the apprehension that the quality of life of the alert patients was being compromised by this arrangement.

To determine if this feeling was a universal one, 10% of all SNF patients were randomly selected for interview (Salamon, 1983). Of these individuals only 24 could take part in the interview due to severe cognitive impairment. Those who were interviewed, however, were almost unanimous in stating their preference for homogeneity of placement. Only one of the 24 patients stated a preference for being on a unit where others had different clinical care needs. It should be noted that interviews were conducted by a Gerontological Society of America post-doctoral fellow, rather than a patient care staff.

THE DEFINITION AND ESTABLISHMENT
OF A SPECIAL CARE UNIT

In addition to the resident and staff interviews, actual and perceived patient care needs were also assessed. This third component of the process included a retrospective analysis of DMS-1 scores[1] for

1978-83, for all HHAR's patients. Additionally, a survey of patient care staff was performed to determine their perception of the extent of the "changing patient profile" at the Home (Salamon, 1983). This was subsequently followed by an assessment of functional levels of all patients using Katz's ADL Scale (Katz et al., 1963). This provided a measure of convergent validity and helped to determine current levels of need for special care, as a result of functional deterioration. It should be noted that the authors believe that it is the severity of the dementing illness or functional psychosis in contrast to its existence, which is the determining variable in placement on a SCU.[2]

When presented with the documented changed needs of patients, the preferences of the more alert and oriented patients, as well as staff's perception of their ability to provide better care, the administration of the HHAR supported the initiative to develop a "SCU" for long-term geriatric patients with dementia. The goal of this initiative was to examine the effectiveness and viability of this model of care for expansion within HHAR and other long-term care institutions.

The development of the SCU required the concurrent operation of two planning processes. The first, a task force chaired by an Administrator, was comprised of relevant Patient Care Department Directors (Medicine, Psychiatry, Social Services, Nursing, Therapeutic and Recreational Therapy), and was responsible for planning for the unit's staffing, therapeutic approaches and environmental modification. A second group of direct care staff coordinated by the Director of Social Services, the designated Admission/Discharge Coordinator, was responsible for the identification of eligible patients, and appropriate transfer protocols.

A SCU for the moderately to severely demented could be made possible at this time only by re-grouping patients within the existing facility. An important issue here is that HHAR did not attempt to build a new unit, change basic physical layout, number of beds or staff to patient ratios within the total institution. This is unlike other SCUs designed for the express purpose of research and demonstration where there are a limited number of patients and high concentrations of staff. Within the context of the current health care climate where reimbursement issues are key, this approach is most replicable.

Planning perspective changed, at this point, from group needs to individual needs and from advocacy to assessment. The initial patient assessment process had identified the specific building in which the highest proportion of moderately to severely functionally impaired and demented patients lived and within which the SCU could best and most logically be developed. It was anticipated that the pool of potential candidates for transfer to the SCU from this building would exceed available capacity of one SCU. Stage two assessments were therefore limited to only this building, which included 3 SNF units. The consistency and patients' familiarity with floor lay-outs within the building (to minimize transfer disorientation) and the simplification of logistics attendant to moving people and their possessions were the key determinants in the selection of the location for the SCU.

All patients within the building were then assessed by the unit social worker and nurse, according to a pre-established and validated criteria set (Salamon et al., 1984). The assessment criteria included a medical diagnosis, documented reports of anti-social behavior, which required greater nursing care and supervision, and a brief evaluation of cognitive functioning. Staff training was organized by and conducted by the clinical psychologist who had designed the instrument (Salamon et al., 1984), a psychiatric social work supervisor and psychiatric nurse clinician.

The joint involvement of the nurse and social worker was based upon research findings at HHAR (Tepper, 1981) which suggested inconsistencies in their assessment perspectives. Nursing staff tended to be more concrete and related to day-to-day function and illness, whereas social work staff were, generally, more optimistic, supportive and focused primarily on the healthy aspects of the patient. Thus the pairing was instituted to coordinate views and maximize objectivity.

The assessment confirmed that the building's first (not ground) floor was most appropriate for conversion. Thirty-three patients (all but 11 currently on the unit) were determined eligible to remain, i.e., requiring special care. This plan, albeit the least aggressive, required moving 22 individuals (i.e., 11 on and 11 off of the unit). Borup (1982) in his review of inter-institutional transfers pointed out, " . . . the enhancement of living and management, coupled with a moderate change in the environment, resulted in a positive effect for patients." The transfer plan which was designed to minimize relocation stress included:

A. Preparation and orientation of both families and patients by social work staff,

B. Transfers limited to one building of consistent floor design,
C. Transfers planned to permit the patient to retain the positive element of his/her immediate environment. For example, a patient in a single room would be transferred to another single room, preferably in the same section of the floor. Compatible roommates, eligible for the same unit, were transferred together to the same room (Gang, & Ackerman, 1983),
D. Transfers, whenever possible were planned with the goal of improving the patient's situation, from their or their families' perspectives. For example, several patients were moved into long-awaited single rooms. Others, were placed in rooms with predictably more compatible roommates then before, or in rooms with a better view, or the favored side of the room.

In working closely with the families, the social workers built upon institutional philosophy and commitment to families as both partners in care and clients in need of social work intervention (Montgomery, 1983). Acknowledgement was given to the view that within institutional long-term care a move to a more intensive level of care is a crisis step for the family (Solomon, 1983). An existing Family Group on the designated SCU, co-led by the unit social worker and nurse helped to ease the transfer and re-location processes. Consistent with this approach, the transfer plan was first introduced at a meeting of this Family Group. Representatives of administration, nursing and social services explained and discussed the background, rationale, goals, as well as the new programs and staffing for the SCU. Families of patients who were to be transferred onto or off of the unit were then contacted, invited to visit the new floors and meet with the staff. Whenever possible, the patients themselves were also involved in the change in the same manner, as a means of participation and preparation.

As is obvious, and was required, much planning focused upon patient and family needs. Department heads and administrative staff expressed concern regarding the need for additional training of staff assigned to SCUs to help deal with the problems of staff anxiety and potential turnover (Holtz, 1982). While initially this was done in a series of general meetings of floor staff, in retrospect, insufficient attention may have been given to planning for staff's needs at the outset. Although the SCU staff had been prepared for this change, and they voiced positive feelings about being part of "something special," the actual effect of a 25% increase in the number of demented patients did create stress and frustration, leading to a temporary decline in staff morale and confidence. Several weeks after the transfers were completed, the psychiatric social work supervisor and the psychiatric nurse clinician were appointed interim project managers to work with unit staff, particularly the nurses aides, to identify specific and general problems whose resolution could help create an atmosphere or milieu that would truly make the unit special.

Daily meetings with the day and evening shifts (lasting 15 minutes) in which all the staff worked together to problem-solve and discuss different cases have made a difference in increasing staff morale and sensitizing them to the special needs of their patients. They have provided a forum that enabled the staff to raise and resolve individual and group problems and have increased the level of trust, self-respect and knowledge among the line staff so that they can deal more effectively with day-to-day issues to improve patient care. Use of a senior psychiatric social worker has made a measurable difference toward open discussions with focused resolution.

MILIEU THERAPY AND THE SPECIAL CARE UNIT

In developing a model for a SCU it was important to consider the environment and activities therein as essential. While there are very few models for the development of such units within traditional nursing homes (Benedict, 1983) literature does exist on making the nursing home environment more comfortable for patients (Hiatt, 1984). The milieu approach in particular (Brink, 1979) was viewed as the essence of care rather than the more traditional medical model. It is noteworthy that even the medical journals (Charatan, 1984; Rabins & Folstein, 1983) emphasize that management of the patient with severe dementia should include elements of organization, including environment and activity, nursing, psychopharmacological treatment, and counseling of the patient's family.

In developing the milieu for this special care unit, the HHAR viewed the environment as an important supportive device rather than indifferent or neutral in providing quality patient care. Cognitively impaired patients are not readily able to adapt to their environments (Lawlor, 1984). Furthermore, they require their environment to be protective, orienting and anxiety reducing as well as supportive of appropriate social stimulation. Environmental manipulations for this SCU including physical adaptations of the skilled nursing unit as well as organizational changes, were therefore essential. Many of these environmental alterations were nominal in cost. Changes included the color coding of doors and hallways to aid confused patients in orientation as well as erecting double-view mirrors to allow staff a better view of the complete unit. The patients, their families and the Social Services and Leisure Time Activities Departments, decorated patients' doors with personal mementos—a useful reminiscence activity as well as an inexpensive orientation tool.

The motherhood and apple pie 24 hour therapeutic milieu was revitalized (Parker & Sommers, 1983). An essential component of this approach was programmatic and staffing consistency. Rotation of nursing and other personnel assignment was discouraged. Staff of all disciplines were assigned and educated as to the specific needs of their patients to heighten their effectiveness and perception as members of the therapeutic team. Nurses aides are viewed as vital members of the team and, in addition to their traditional tasks, are assigned to on-the-unit activities including therapy, exercise, and crafts activities. This approach increased their understanding of the reasons for the activities, provided education in patient-support techniques, extended the effectiveness of the programs beyond their limited activity slot through on-going integration and teaching and developed a means of support to non-nursing personnel.

Daily on the unit programming is now consistent. Activity times are fixed thus enhancing time orientation for the patient (Pannala, 1984). A typical day might include:

7:00 am - 10:30 am	Breakfast, activities of daily living, Medical and Clinic appointments.
10:30 am - 11:15 am	Sensory integration group - Occupational Therapy (OT)
11:15 am - 12:00 noon	Adaptive sports activities - Leisure Time Activities (LTA).
12:00 noon - 2:00 pm	Lunch, toileting, rest time.

1:45 pm - 2:30 pm	Exercise programming including upper extremities - rotation by OT, Physical Therapy (PT), LTA.
	Walking groups - PT, Social Services (SS).
2:30 pm - 3:15 pm	Active socialization Activities (e.g., Poetry and discussion, crafts and reminiscence). - LTA.
3:30 pm - 4:15 pm	Communication groups - (i.e., verbal games, coffee klatches). Rotation by LTA, Audiology and Speech Pathology.
5:30 pm -	Dinner

Evening activities that are more passive, such as music, are conducted between the hours of six and eight p.m.

To the extent possible, programs are brought to the unit, rather than patients brought to the activity. We have found that this reduces anxiety about leaving the familiarity of the unit and maximizes staff resources.

Physical activity is considered an important component of the daily routine. The benefits of these activities for improved circulation, prevention of urinary tract infections, fecal impactions and contractures, and improved sleeping habits have been noted in the literature and corroborated by staff experience (Brink, 1979; Charatan, 1984; Lawlor, 1984). Similarly, the inclusion of traditional reality orientation activities within all group settings combined with visible calendars and reality orientation boards enhances individual and group orientation. We share the belief that orientation is important for individuals with both reversible and irreversible organic impairments (Parker & Somers, 1983).

EVALUATION AND IMPACT

The adaptation of a 44 bed unit to make it safe, secure and appropriate for providing specialized care for difficult to manage psychogeriatric patients is, surprisingly, not a costly one. Expenses related to physical plant modifications, are, as indicated earlier, of minimal cost. A perceptible increase in expense may exist in relationship to staffing. Of the models for specialized care that have been reported, suggested staffing is intensive with as many as nine care providers for 10 to 12 patients (Parker & Somers, 1983). Few facilities have the resources to develop such an intense demonstration project. Staffing in long term care facilities is determined by the acuity level of patient care needs. By increasing the overall need on a particular unit the level of staffing need also increases. Nonetheless staffing can only be increased within the parameters allowed by reimbursement rates and very high staff to patient ratios cannot be anticipated. What can be expected is that a fair division of labor for care providers will be maintained, and that a shifting of overall institutional staff to reflect units with "higher" and "lower" patient care needs will be accomplished. Improved standards of performance can be set and met through the provision of education, support, motivational techniques and morale building.

The patients on a SCU have distinct needs which require a level of insight and understanding different than that required on regular skilled nursing units. This can be communicated and learned through specialized training. The provision of this training is a costly but necessary element in establishing a SCU. As noted previously, daily 15 minute meetings of staff with nursing and psychiatric social work supervisors allowed staff to ventilate and explore the feelings associated with working on such a unit. Discussion of general principles of dealing with patients who have special needs as well as case-specific reviews also gave staff the opportunity to develop the understanding and strategies necessary to deal with these patients. Additionally, all unit staff including the unit physician, nurses, aides, social workers, housekeepers and therapists attend bi-monthly community grand rounds.

A review of process notes of the daily meetings, as well as the community grand round meetings, indicates staff's increasing ability to accurately report difficulties on the unit, better understanding for the patients and their behavior, and improved skills and abilities to interact with the patients. Staff on the SCU are satisfied with their unit and unanimously report that they are better able to provide care now that all the patients are at the same level of functional need. Staff on the other units also report a better ability to care for their patients when they are at a homogeneous level of care need. Patients on the remaining units have reported, through the Resident Council, that they are pleased with the change and have urged a continuation of the development of homogeneous units.

To determine the actual benefits to the patients residing on the special care unit a variety of secondary measures were utilized. A preliminary evaluation of the number of accidents which took place on the unit indicates that for the six months prior to and for four months following, the development of this SCU the average number of monthly accidents decreased from 16 to 10. The use of psychotropic medications is, on the average, no different on the SCU than any other unit. Patients are free to wander safely on the SCU, therefore, the use of physical restraints has decreased as well as reported cases of significant acting out behavior by the patients. A behavioral assessment of the number of screams on the SCU (measured daily at the same time) indicates that they have diminished from 18 to 20 per five minute period, during the initial weeks of the establishment of the SCU to an average of three to six six months later. Anecdotal reports suggest that the screams have also diminished in intensity.

Two patients, known throughout the facility for constantly screaming most of the day, no longer do so. Staff has learned how to deal effectively with these individuals. Another patient known for her severe confusion, isolation, non-communication and constant wandering has begun to take part in music activities. A pianist prior to the onset of her illness she had for many years refused to acknowledge her former talent. On the SCU she requested (independently) the right to play piano. Now she does so regularly both for her own as well as all the other patients' enjoyment. While the project is still in its early stages and the evaluation is primarily based on slightly more than first impressions, it would appear that there are a number of benefits for the patients who reside on the SCU. They experience less traumas, are apparently more comfortable in their present setting, have greater "freedom" and minimized use of restraints.

ROLE OF THE SOCIAL WORKER

The involvement of social workers in the conceptualization, planning and development stages of the SCU, often in key decision making and organizational roles, is viewed as having had an important and effective impact on the positive manner in which this sizeable change was accomplished. It suggested that social workers can and must be considered or make themselves considered an instrumental and necessary part of any such institutional change. Traditionally, the effectiveness and validity of the social worker has been rooted in his or her relationship with the client. In long-term care, the client has primarily been the elderly patient, and the preferred modality was traditional counseling; however, as the composition of the population in such facilities becomes increasingly skewed toward the cognitively impaired, the role of the social worker must be expanded to include working more actively with institutional systems and staff which can have the greatest impact upon the establishment and maintenance of a positive, supportive, and pleasurable environment. On a SCU, a changed proportion of the social workers time may be spent in auxiliary functions (Silverstone, & Weiss, 1983), with significant others in support of interdisciplinary efforts on the patient's behalf as well as related collaborative planning efforts. Increased involvement with families, in helping them to understand the aging and daycare process to enhance their relationship with the patients.

It is perhaps bold to postulate such a broad set of responsibilities for social workers when in many parts of the country the professional social worker's presence in long-term care facilities reflects little more than paper compliance rather than an active and viable role in institutional policy and planning (Garner, 1980). Yet our experience in establishing this SCU suggests that such a viable presence can make a real difference in the manner in which care is organized and provided for the most vulnerable and fastest growing segment of society.

NOTES

1. The DMS-1 is the weighted assessment tool, to determine eligibility for (Medicaid) admission and continued stay in nursing homes in New York State. Functional, mental and physical status were evaluated by nursing personnel.
2. The term "Special Care Unit" was chosen rather than psycho-geriatric unit to minimize stigma and anxiety for patients and their families.

REFERENCES

Ablowitz, M. (1983) (letter to the editor), Pairing Rational and Demented Patients in Long-Term Care Facilities, *Journal of the American Geriatrics Society*, 31:10, 627-28.
Benedict, S.P. (1983) The decision to establish a closed psychiatric unit: Some ethical and administrative considerations. *The Journal of Long-Term Care Administration.* 22-26.

Borup, J.H. (1982) The effects of varying levels of inter-institutional environment. *The Gerontologist*, 22, 409-417.

Borus, J.F. (1981) Deinstitutionalization of the chronically mentally ill. *New England Journal of Medicine*, 305, 339, 342.

Bowker, L.H. (1982) *Humanizing Institutions for the Aged*, Lexington, Mass. Lexington Books.

Brink, T.L. (1979) *Geriatric Psychotherapy*. Human Sciences Press, New York, New York.

Butler, R.N., & Lewis, M.I. (1982) *Aging and Mental Health: Positive Psychosocial and Biomedical Approaches, 3rd Ed.*, St. Louis, C.V. Mosby.

Charatan, B. (1984) Caring for your nursing home patients, *Geriatric Consultants*, July/August, 1984, 14-15.

Curtis, R.E. & Bartlett, L.R. (1984) Long-Term Care Squeezes State Budgets, *Generations*, Fall, 1984, 22-25.

Daum, M. (1982) Preference for age-homogeneous versus age-heterogeneous social interaction. *Journal of Gerontological Social Work*, 4, 41-55.

Gang, R. and Ackerman, J.O. (1983) (letter to the editor) Pairing Rational and Demented Patients in Long-Term Care Facilities, *Journal of the American Geriatrics Society, 31*, 627-28.

Garner, J.D. & Mercer, S.O. (1980) Social work practice in long-term care facilities: Implications of the Current Model. *Journal of Gerontological Social Work*, 3, 2, 71-77.

Getzel, G.S. & Mellor, M.J. (1982) Introduction: Overview of Gerontological Social Work in Long-Term Care, *Journal of Gerontological Social Work*, 5, 1-6.

Goldfarb, A.I. (1973) *Aged Patients in Long-Term Care Facilities*, National Institute of Mental Health, Rockville, Md.

Hiatt, L.G. (1980) Conveying the substance of images: Interior design in long-term care. *Contemporary Administrator for Long Term Care*, 4, 17-23.

Holtz, G.A. (1982) Nurses' aides in nursing homes: Why are they satisfied? *Journal of Gerontological Nursing*, 8, 265-271.

Katz, S., Ford, A.B., Moskowitz, R.W., Jackson, B.A. and Jaffee, M.W. (1983) Studies of illness in the aged: The index of ADL: A standardized measure of biological and psychosocial function. *Journal of the American Medical Association, 185*, 94.

Koff, T.H. (1982) *Long-Term Care: An Approach to Serving the Frail Elderly*, Boston. Little, Brown & Co.

Lawlor, A. (1984) Adjusting to the special needs of dementia patients. *Today's Nursing Home*, August, 6-7.

Montgomery, R.J.V. (1983) Staff-family relations and institutional care policy. *Journal of Gerontological Social Work*, 6, 25-37.

Panella, J.R., McDowell, F.H. (1984) Day Care for Dementia. The Burke Rehabilitation Center Auxiliary.

Parker, C., & Somers, C. (1983) Reality Orientation on a geropsychiatric unit. *Geriatric Nursing, 5*, 163-165.

Pavur, E.J., Jr., & Smith, P.C. (1983) Absenteeism, turnover and an in-service program. In M.A. Smyer, & M. Gatz. *Mental Health and Aging*, Beverly Hills: Sage Publications.

Rabins, P.V. & Folstein, M.F. (1983) The dementia patient: Evaluation and Care: *Geriatrics*, 38:3,99-106.

Rosow, I. (1974) *Socialization to Old Age*. Berkeley, California, University of California Press.

Silverstone, B. & Burack-Weiss, A. (1982) The Social Work Function in Nursing Homes and Home Care, *Journal of Gerontological Social Work*, 5:1/2, 7-34.

Salamon, M.J. (1983) Matching Services to Long-Term Care Need. Unpublished manuscript, Hebrew Home for the Aged at Riverdale.

Salamon, M.J., Grossman, H.D., & Weiner, A.S. (1984) Development of Criteria for Psychogeriatric Placement. Paper presented at the 37th Annual Meeting of the Gerontological Society of America, San Antonio, Texas.

Solomon, R. (1983) Serving families of the institutionalized aged: The four crises, *Gerontological Social Work*, 5, 83 96.

Stotsky, B.A. (1970) *The Nursing Home and the Psychiatric Patient:* New York: Appleton Century Crofts.

Tepper, L. (1981) The Use of Subjective and Informant Reports to Assess Cognitive Status and Functional Performance of Geriatric Patients in a Long-Term Care Facility, Unpublished manuscript, Hebrew Home for the Aged at Riverdale.

Tobin, S.S., Davidson, S.M., & Sack, A. (1976) Effective social services for older Americans. Institute of Gerontology, University of Michigan/Wayne State University.

Zimmer, J.G., Watson, N., & Treat, A. (1984) Behavioral problems among patients in skilled nursing facilities, *American Journal of Public Health*, 74: 10, 1118-1121.

Adjusting to a Residential Facility for Older Persons: A Child's Perspective

Bernard Reisman

I've helped my four children getting started in nursery school, elementary school and summer camps. I've gone through their farewells before going off to college and trips overseas. None of these difficult parenting experiences was as emotionally trying as the recent experience I have had in helping my elderly father adjust to living in a residential facility for older persons.

My father is 84 years of age. As well as such a diagnosis can be made, the doctors say dad is in the "early stages of Alzheimer's Disease." About five years ago he began to show symptoms of memory loss and uncertainty in finding his way around. His physical health is good; he is cheerful and enjoys being with people. When his wife (my mother) died a few months ago it was clear he would not be able to manage living alone in their apartment. My wife and I and my brother and his wife experimented with having father live at our homes. Since all of us work, those arrangements were problematic as we realized that he needed constant care. Further he soon became bored and we became exhausted as we tried to figure out how to provide stimulation and to respond to the constancy of his needs and his oft-repeated questions.

So the decision was made to find an appropriate residential facility for older persons. Father was not eager to live in a "Home," saying such places were for "those old cocka-doodles." Yet he would acknowledge that he couldn't live at his former apartment and he recognized that living with his sons presented problems. Despite extended discussions about the pluses inherent in living in one of the residences for older persons, and visits to see the wonderful

Bernard Reisman is Director, Hornstein Program in Jewish Communal Service, Brandeis University, Waltham, MA 02254.

91

resources available, when my brother and I finally brought dad for his first day at Lakeview,* he was not enthusiastic about what lay ahead.

Now some months later dad has made a moderately good adjustment to Lakeview. With his illness, under the most optimal conditions, one would expect problems not only in terms of the initial adjustment to such a major change in life situation, but in the day to day struggles to keep a coherent hold on reality. Our family is in full agreement that the placement in the residence is in dad's best interest, now and in the future. The constancy of basic care in an environment custom designed for people like him is something even dad seems to have recognized as good for him. In the first weeks he spoke of the place as a "jail." Recently he has occasionally referred to Lakeview as a "hotel," and has at least accepted the fact that this is where he now lives.

What led me to write this article was to say something about what I have learned about helping a parent accommodate to such a transition. I know the opportunity to express myself also has a cathartic benefit for me. I hope that my observations may be of help to the people who are responsible for running residential settings for older persons and to other families who have, or will have, parents or relatives in such settings.

THE 4 R'S OF ADJUSTMENT

My wife is an early childhood educator. I remember her constantly stressing, with parents of young children just starting pre-school, the critical importance of the parents' presence in those first days, until the child seemed ready to manage alone. The principle was that to the extent the parent was consistently available to help the child through the initial adjustment, the child's long term adjustment, except in rare cases, was assured. Our family agreed the principle equally applied to an older person beginning to live in a residence for older persons.

Because of a fortunate coincidence of a sabbatical leave at the time of my father's placement, I had the time to be available to aid in the process. I am convinced that my presence and that of my brother

---

*A pseudonym for a community supported facility for older persons in a major urban location.

and our wives during those first weeks contributed significantly to my father's adjustment.

As I have thought about that adjustment process I became aware of four factors, which I identified as "the 4 R's of adjustment." The first is *Reassurance.*

I spent most of the first three days at Lakeview with my father. By the third day I thought it was time for weaning. As my father got ready for dinner that evening I said goodbye to him and told him I wouldn't see him again for several days. He was somewhat apprehensive. I assured him that he had done very well those first few days, that I and the rest of the family were proud of the way he had managed, and I knew he would continue to do well. "I hope you're right," he replied, "but I don't have your confidence." Despite his uncertainties, he was pleased to have the encouragement and support.

He frequently would ask in those first days, "Are you sure this is the right place for me?" The family's consistent, unwavering, affirmative responses at least didn't add to his own ambivalence. It was also helpful to dad to know that we appreciated the effort he was going through in trying to adjust to his new living arrangements. And while he had (and continues to have) uncertainties, he drew reassurance from our confidence in him and from our physical presence. That we were there with him helped dissipate a major source of his anxiety—that he would be abandoned at the Home. Our presence further assured him that we could be counted on to help him to cope with the succession of new experiences that lay ahead.

Which brings me to the second factor, *Routes.* As is the case with people with Alzheimers there is much uncertainty about getting places. Several months before mom died she reported that dad no longer would go to the grocery store, a block from their apartment, to pick up milk, bread, and simple groceries, as he had always done. He was unsure that he would find his way back. He had lived in that neighborhood for over 25 years. Imagine his confusion coming to live in a large, strange institution with several wings, each with many floors.

An activity which occupied much of our time together the first days at Lakeview was going over the important routes in his new environment. First we located the basic bathroom in his room and then another strategically located bathroom outside the dining room (the bathroom is a sanctuary for dad.) Getting from his room on the 6th floor to the 1st floor dining room was another route which we traversed several times. Given that dad's capacity to retain data is now limited, information needs to be presented clearly and regularly reinforced. Having one of your children as an almost around the clock tutor helps. This is not a stranger with whom one has to make yet another adjustment. This aide comes with instant acceptance, trust, and a shared language. Together we identified ways of making the routes easier to remember, in some cases, by establishing familiar associations with memories from dad's past.

"Dad, how can you remember your table number in the dining room—number 37?"

"Thirty-seven, 37, oh that will be easy, that was the number of my Union—local 37."

"Wow, local 37—table 37, piece of cake!"

Some routes could be rendered more accessible by "road markings." Complicating dad's problems with finding his way is that he has very poor vision. When he gets up at night to go to the bathroom he does not put on his glasses. That makes finding the bathroom and getting back to bed an even greater challenge. One important marker we established with his roommate was the agreement to keep the bathroom light on at night. One of those first nights that wasn't enough help. Dad drifted out of his room and went to the bathroom in someone else's room and frightened the other resident as well as himself. When dad was living in my home I came upon the idea of using chairs to mark the route from his room to the bathroom. An adaptation for his room at Lakeview was to post a big octagonal red STOP sign on the inside of his door. We rehearsed several times the meaning of the STOP sign. So far, at least, it has succeeded in keeping dad from leaving his room in the middle of the night.

In a similar vein we worked together on the third R—the *Routines* of the residence, or to continue the alliteration—learning the ropes and rhythms of life at Lakeview. On a personal care level: remembering to shave and brush teeth every day, figuring out ways of getting a regular change of clothes, putting dirty clothes in the laundry bag, and getting clean clothing reasonably organized in the closet and bureau. The objective was to coach dad in establishing behaviors, through repetition and reinforcement, needed to adapt to his new environment. To the extent he acheives some mastery of these routines his self confidence is bolstered and he is encouraged in his capacities to cope with his new life situation.

We knew it would be important for dad's self-image that he keep up his personal appearance. We consistently monitored and coached him to dress neatly, shave and bathe regularly. We discovered that his personal appearance was an important determinant of the response of staff and other residents to him. Regularly people would comment approvingly about dad's appearance. "He is very neat." "Your father always looks so nice." At the same time they would contrast his appearance with that of others who were disheveled and unkempt, and who tended to be ostracized.

Then there is the issue of how to fill those large blocks of time between meals and before going to sleep. For those residents with either an interest in television watching or a low energy level, this is not a problem. Neither of those conditions apply to my father. He needs to do things and be with people. When he has such opportunities he is at his best. He feels good about himself. Left to his own resources he becomes bored and depressed. This routine proved to be our most intractable problem. The only way dad could avail himself, on a consistent basis, of the activities offered at different locations throughout the Home would be with the aid of one of the staff. And this leads us to our last R: *Relationships.*

Perhaps the most important of the four areas of adjustment in which the family's involvement has been helpful is establishing connections with the other residents and the staff—two new and vital groups of people in my father's life.

As one considers the nature of this adjustment one can appreciate its difficulties as well as its importance. On entering the Home my father was confronted with the task of taking on what, in effect, was an instant family and homestead, and at a time when his adaptive capacities were weakened by the combination of the loss of his most critical family relationship, his wife, and by his illness. The helping presence of his children lessened the overwhelming nature of the task and extended dad's resources. Relationships slowly began to get established and to provide their own healing. What could have been a "too much to cope with" experience, leading to a sense of defeat and retreat, instead was converted to an experience in which dad felt some sense of mastery. With our support dad reached out to engage himself with the other people—residents and staff. They in turn were responsive to dad's initiatives and as a result tended to reinforce his resolve to make it at Lakeview. It helped to have the friendly greetings and banter with the several staff members and the frequent encouraging words from veteran residents: "You'll get along fine here, it's just tough in the beginning." or "It's better here than with children. It takes a little while, but you'll get used to it. We all did.''

How did we help these relationships to develop? In the most basic sense we took the initiative to introduce dad to the other people. The pattern of interpersonal relationships among the residents is that people coexist with each other. Because everyone is so attentive to their own personal needs and because there is so much transience among the residents in the living units, the veteran residents have neither the emotional energy nor the inclination to reach out to the newcomer. By our initiative we surmount these obstacles and open the prospect for future interactions. Also, our frequent presence and interest in the other residents is transferred to dad's attractiveness as a potential "friend." We become accessible to them through dad. They enjoy chatting with us and having our attention. After an extended chat one afternoon in the lounge (which drew attention away from the ever playing TV), one of the residents remarked with enthusiasm, "One conversation is better than a month's pills."

That his children were very caring of dad was noticed with approval by residents and staff. Sometimes they remarked on it to us; other times we overheard observations such as this comment from one resident to another: "Isn't it nice how his children watch over him." The residents seemed to identify with dad and to vicariously experience our caring. For the staff, that we cared and were patient with our father made it easier for them to extend themselves in a similar fashion with him. Such a staff response can be best understood by considering the converse: the situation when little or no family interest is expressed in a resident. A staff reaction, likely without consciousness, might well be to reason, "If his own family doesn't worry about him, why should I?"

We made it a point to meet and talk with as many staff as we could: aides, orderlies, nurses, social workers, recreation staff. . . . With some we just had a friendly chat; with some we talked about dad and his background and interests; and with others we exchanged information about dad's habits and idiosyncrasies with an eye toward how best to manage him. With all staff we sought to convey the message that we took them seriously and appreciated their role. Obviously staff feel good when recognized for their helping efforts. It is reasonable to assume that this good feeling carried over in their attitudes to dad.

Dad brought to our attention another benefit, from his perspective, of our interactions with staff. He seemed comforted by the fact that his natural family was communicating with the new care-givers in his life. This visible collaboration made it easier for dad to conceive of staff as possible surrogate kin. He expressed such a reaction at a meeting involving him, his social worker and me. The social worker asked dad how he felt about our meeting together. He replied, "I like it. It makes me feel that everyone is trying to help me and I want to do my best to please you."

One final aspect of our interaction with staff was our functioning as dad's advocate. We would push the system—staff and/or operating procedures—when, in our judgment dad wasn't getting the best care. From the perspective of the Home we might be wrong or unreasonable, and in such cases they would ignore us. In most instances our assuming the advocate's role resulted in "the squeaking wheel getting the oil." Our "client's" interests were well served. At the same time, to the extent that our ideas and perspectives helped the system become more sensitized to one resident it is quite possible the system became more responsive to other residents.

It may be helpful to describe in somewhat greater detail the advocacy role in operation, focusing on an area in which we have invested much energy and the one area in which we have been disappointed with the Lakeview Home. Dad was placed on an Intermediate unit at Lakeview, which means that the level of care is not as intensive as "Skilled Nursing" but more individualized than in a "Health Related" unit. This seemed like an ideal placement for someone like dad who can be self-directing, but needs occasional staff supervision. The problem was, as discussed earlier, the large blocks of time with nothing to do and virtually no staff time made available to help residents constructively utilize this time. For dad's well-being we felt our prime priority was to get him involved in the activities.

There is a reasonably good program of recreational activities offered at Lakeview, at least as these are outlined in the daily schedule posted on bulletin boards throughout the Home. But the dilemma is how to get the residents to the activities. The combination of lethargy and as in my father's case, inability to get to and from the activities unaided, make the activities "near and yet so far" for the vast majority of the residents. The task seemed simple enough: go over the day's scheduled activities with dad and decide what interested him and then get someone to take him there. We discovered that when the system is accustomed to a certain way of doing things it doesn't change easily (if at all). Our eagerness and enterprising spirits were (and continue to be) pushed to the limits on the issue of getting someone to accompany dad to recreation programs. The Head Nurse of the floor is the key person who controls the use of aides and orderlies. She typically responded to our requests for a staff-person to accompany dad by telling of the problems she faces with never having enough staff to keep up with meeting the basic physical requirements of her residents. Also she had to use the orderlies to line up the residents for their regular distribution of pills and to get them to their many appointments at the Clinic. "Would she," I gently persisted one day, "consider having an orderly help dad go to an exercise class for his mental well-being just as orderlies help residents take their pills or go to the Clinic for their physical well-being?" She answered somewhat impatiently, "You should really speak to the social worker."

That afternoon I managed to get an appointment with the social worker who supervises the 6th floor Intermediate Unit (she's based on the 1st floor). The following is the pertinent excerpt of our discussion:

"I was thinking Ms. B it could be helpful to many of the other residents on the 6th floor besides my father, if they could get to some of the recreation activities. Couldn't one of the orderlies make it a point each day to point out to the residents what was planned and encourage them to attend."

"Well Mr. Reisman that is not something the orderlies could do. You're trying to make them into social directors."

On reflection, I realized that broadening the job definition of the orderly was what I had in mind. Since the orderlies have the most contact and are most familar with the residents, shouldn't they be encouraged to take initiatives rather than function only when and as directed by a supervisor? Might not more autonomy foster more of the orderlies' natural caring instincts and more responsiveness to the residents' daily living needs? And might not such an enhanced definition of their role have a positive effect on the orderlies' level of job satisfaction and such perennial problems as burn-out and staff turnover?

As I began to raise such "far out" issues the social worker suggested we were getting into matters which were out of her control. "Maybe you ought to make an appointment with my supervisor." I did. She listened sympathetically and said: "These are very interesting ideas which I will try to get on the agenda of our next interdepartmental staff meeting."

Dad was still bored and only very sporadically getting to recreation programs.

One final chapter in this episode of advocacy. I discovered in a casual converation with the head nurse that for several weeks dad had been receiving a tranquillizing medication "to deal with his restlessness." Leave aside for another article the issue of involvement of the family in decisions to administer drugs. Suffice for now for me to describe the extension of the advocate's role in a phone conversation I initiated with the Home's psychiatrist. The psychiatrist described the nature and dosage of the medication (which was quite mild) which he prescribed for dad. I told the doctor that in recent days we had noticed that dad seem uncharacteristically lethargic. The doctor appreciated the observation and indicated he was monitoring dad's response to the level of medication and such a reaction might indicate a need to lower the dosage. He planned to see dad later that day. Pleasantly surprised by the psychiatrist's responsiveness, I offered one other suggestion: "Could you prescribe Occupational Therapy or Recreation for dad as another way of dealing with his restlessness?" He responded, "Hm, that's an interesting idea. Why not? I'll follow up on your suggestion with the staff. Why don't you call me in two weeks?"

A persistent advocate occasionally gets unanticipated results.

I began this description of the process of helping settle my father in a home for older persons by saying it was an emotionally trying experience. It hurts to watch a once vibrant and able man becoming frightened and passive. It hurts to watch dad amble through the dining room as he searches for his assigned table, each time uncertain that he will get to the right place. It hurts to find in his pockets little scraps of paper on which he has scribbled his room number, evidence of his struggle to retain the information needed to survive in his new situation. It hurts to have to bathe and dress the man who once bathed and dressed me. It hurts when he cries, apologizing for "becoming a burden." In sum, it hurts to know that the man on whom I used to depend with total confidence now is dependent upon me. We have reversed roles: he the child, I the parent. With one important and hurtful difference: One can look forward with optimism to a child growing and becoming a source of pride; with dad we know our efforts are at best very temporary and inevitably the future means continuing decline. Indeed, as you read this it is likely some of the hard achieved adjustments I have described will have evaporated.

But it would hurt very much more, as dad embarks on this next phase of his life, if we didn't do all that we reasonably can to increase the likelihood that he might live out his days comfortably and with some dignity.

Family Respite
for the
Elderly Alzheimer's Patient

Donald L. Spence, PhD
Dulcy B. Miller, MSAM

ABSTRACT. Respite services for families of Alzheimer's patients are quite new. Conceptualization of the issues involved as well as the objectives for program application can best be developed in response to varied experience. The family respite program described in this paper has helped to identify the importance of patient assessment in relation to the services offered as well as the role of the nursing home in providing such services. By placing this description in the context of social policy, community values and family expectations one begins to understand the importance of respite in helping to maintain the frail elderly in their own homes.

Respite is a relatively new service in the long term care of elderly individuals. With the introduction of the demonstration projects which attempt to channel services to clients in the community as an alternative to institutional care (Eggert et al., 1980; Hodgson & Quinn, 1980; U.S. Senate, 1984), as well as the basic change in policy which has decentralized services and responsibilities (U.S. Senate, 1984; Morris, 1981), there has been an attempt to develop and to improve services which can serve this function. Several reasons make this more difficult than one might expect.

First, there is a problem in the conceptualization of what respite is and what it should accomplish. It is not a service directed toward the health needs of the individual being cared for, but a service directed toward the needs of family care-givers. In the British system this has been accepted and is supported in their social service values. Government has a responsibility to provide services generally to

Donald L. Spence is affiliated with the University of Rhode Island and Dulcy B. Miller with the Nathan Miller Center for Nursing Care.

assist society in achieving collective objectives with respite programs organized and administered through the local social service departments (Carter, 1981). In the American value system social services are viewed as welfare, as a stigma to be avoided (Estes, 1979). Consequently, even under the most liberal administrations, social service programs are seldom offered to the able bodied. An exception is the New York State Respite Demonstration Project.

Chapter 767 of the 1981 Laws of the State of New York authorized a three year demonstration of respite services. Seven agencies throughout New York received funds to administer their proposed respite projects with one of the seven receiving additional funds to assist clients in paying for the services (Perdue, 1984). The final evaluation of these projects was due in January of 1985. Interim Reports submitted to the Governor and State Legislature by the New York Department of Social Services provide descriptions of the various projects and their experiences to date. Although respite in these projects is seen as relief for care-givers from the stresses of providing constant care, the underlying purpose is to deter institutionalization.

A second problem can be seen in relation to the expense of providing respite services. In the instance of persons on Medicaid where the government already has financial responsibility, respite services are viewed as part of the total costs involved in providing care. If a family is willing to care for a loved one as the result of their loved one being supported by community services: day care, chore services, etc., and the total costs are 75 percent or less than institutional care, waivers enable payment for these services (U.S. Senate, 1984), but the services are directed toward the client and not the family. Since the client is sick or handicapped, the regulations governing most of these health related services make them less than cost effective as organized respite programs. In the British experience, residential respite services are provided at a cost considerably less than the average intermediate care facility. They are not designed to provide health services but to relieve families one day per week or for a family holiday period once or twice a year. If health services are required, they are provided independent of the respite program (Liddiard, 1980).

Respite services in a health facility are appropriate for clients whose health status demands professional supervision or skilled nursing services. Under these circumstances, one would expect the costs to parallel those provided for continuing residents. However, the organization of a service directed toward the family care-giver of a functioning older individual should provide respite at a cost more consistent with the British experience. Before this can happen, a number of questions need answers. What is the optimal size and organization in relation to appropriate care and economic efficiency? What staff are required and how should they be trained? What is the role of respite in the prevention or delay of institutionalization and/or in preparation for needed institutional care? What are the differences in objectives for clients of respite as opposed to continuing care services? The Nathan Miller Center for Nursing Care has developed a pilot respite program to begin answering these questions.

The Family Respite for the Elderly program was designed to provide temporary relief for families caring for a loved one with Alzheimer's disease or a related disorder at home. Participation was to follow a pattern established for the admission of patients to the Center for Nursing Care. This involves a home or hospital assessment of prospective candidates for admission to determine the patient's functional status and the care plan anticipated in providing for the respite resident.

Originally the service was conceptualized as an apartment with a live-in housekeeper. Since potential clients were living at home without professional assistance, it was assumed that the only care required would be supervision and companionship which could be provided by the housekeeper in an apartment neighboring on the property of a skilled nursing facility (SNF). The second person admitted to the apartment, however, demonstrated that the trauma of relocation can itself precipitate problems that only the close supervision of professionally trained personnel can handle. This experience pointed to the need to evaluate potential clients on the premises of the services to be provided to better anticipate the response of the client to the limited stay. We will return to this point later. For now we need to describe the project to date, the patients and their families, the services to be provided including staff roles and finally the criteria by which to evaluate the experience.

THE PROJECT TO DATE

The project started as an outgrowth of interest expressed by the Alzheimer's Disease and Related Disorders Association, Inc. (A.D.R.D.A.), Westchester Chapter. Responding to this interest,

Dulcy Miller, Administrative Director of The Nathan Miller Center for Nursing Care, decided to develop an apartment for respite care adjacent to the White Plains Center Division. The apartment was refinished and furnished during the spring of 1984 and admitted its first respite client in July.

To date ten families have participated in the respite program, four in the nursing home and six in the apartment. Of the ten care-receivers, two presented with early Alzheimer's disease and four, more advanced. Their mean age, 79, is somewhat younger than the average skilled nursing patient. The number of women and men were equal at five each. Spouses were the principal care-giver for half, with a sister-in-law, a granddaughter, a daughter, and two sons accounting for the other five. Respite stays ranged from four to thirty days with most in the two week category. The four day client in the apartment returned for a second stay lasting eight days and has reserved space for a third stay. One nursing home respite patient and two from the apartment have been readmitted for long term care. The purpose of the respite was to provide vacation time for six of the care-givers, a temporary arrangement for another while permanent arrangements were being made, rest and relaxation for two spouses, and the opportunity to prepare for a move to Florida for another spouse.

The Westchester Chapter, A.D.R.D.A. is still working through the issues of their relation to respite services generally. They have arranged short term home help and have access to day services at Burke Rehabilitation Center. Beside these services, the respite program at the apartment and the White Plains Center are the extent of current services. Their experience to date would indicate that the home care is not being utilized. This is consistent with other explorations indicating that without an adequate promotional effort, families are reluctant to try what is essentially a disruption in a working routine for as little as four hours of respite in a week. The 1981 Inspector General's service delivery assessment of Medicare's home health program reported no sign of active client participation in soliciting home health services (U.S. Senate, 1982).

Policy with respect to the duration and extent of support are currently being worked out in a Chapter committee and will be referred to the Board of the Westchester Chapter, A.D.R.D.A. for approval when the details have been worked out. Since the members of this committee have all had personal experience with an Alzheimer's family member, the results will undoubtedly reflect a thoughtful approach to a very difficult problem.

THE PATIENTS AND THEIR FAMILIES

The short term placement of the respite client as contrasted to continuing placement makes for a very different set of problems in providing for him/her and in relating to his/her family. In a long-term placement the SNF and its staff become fixed parts of the network of relationships within which the resident's course of illness is pursued as well as important role players in the course of family development for those significant to the resident. The term "family" is used in this context in its broadest conception to include those friendship relationships within which people meet their socioemotional needs. The evidence to support this conception can be seen in two ways. First, it is evident in the way in which family members try to manipulate the SNF and its staff so that the care provided becomes an extension of the significant other in meeting his/her own needs rather than the needs of the resident (Bernstein & Sharkey, 1979; Miller, 1976). Second, it is evident in the way family members become part of the SNF, defining for themselves roles in the nursing home which in some cases even survive their loved one. (Two of the more active members of the family organization that supports Center activities are the "family" of someone now deceased for over 3 years.) In the long-term placement, there is time to identify and to resolve or work on those issues specific to an individual family. With the short term respite client, this is not possible.

The best that can be hoped for in the short term placement is that the client can fit into an existing routine. In the relationship of the respite program to the SNF we are trying to provide maximum flexibility. Instead of the complex process of readjustments required in the continuing placement, however, the burden is on the client and his/her family to accept what the program can offer. This places a significant demand on assessing the client and some real flexibility on the part of families to view the placement in specific and limited terms. Since there will be relocation issues that impact the client, the goal of respite must be seen in terms of what it provides for family caretakers (Carter, 1981). If the caretaker's expectations are inconsistent with what the program can provide, it may produce a less than satisfactory experience.

One of the families to be served by the respite program was a widowed mother and her unmarried daughter who lived together in an apartment. The mother had become progressively confused and disoriented over the past four years. Initially the daughter wanted to try the service to see how her mother would respond. When the four day stay worked effectively she made reservations for the first real vacation she had had in the four years, a week's trip to Bermuda. During the longer stay we discovered that the mother experienced nocturnal wandering to an extent that endangered her safety. In the shorter visit the housekeeper had seen this agitation but had assumed it was due to the newness of the experience. After the longer stay it was clear that the behavior was a manifestation of the disease process.

The daughter was aware of her mother's agitated behavior and was disappointed that we were unable to handle her in the apartment. The daughter had initially responded by locking her mother in her room when she went to bed or in the apartment when the daughter was away at work or shopping. However, as the disease progressed it had become necessary to employ a companion for the mother during the times the daughter was away. The main issue to the daughter was the difference in the cost between the apartment and the SNF. Even with the help she was receiving from the Westchester Chapter, A.D.R.D.A., she knew that her ability to use the more expensive respite services would be limited.

SERVICES TO BE PROVIDED

An apartment building within the same block as the SNF was finished to provide a ground floor apartment with two separate-room sleeping arrangements and a live-in housekeeper who would provide company and prepare required meals. Guests would be encouraged to use the Center's facilities and join in group activities by walking next door to the SNF. When the two respite clients have different needs or expectations, a second aide would be available during the day to ensure that each person has the supervision he/she requires in relation to his/her program of care.

The apartment has been refinished and furnished to provide a home-away-from-home atmosphere and ambiance. There is a living room with television and comfortable traditional furnishings to provide for relaxed living. The eat-in kitchen is modern with all the necessary equipment to provide for the needs of guests. A separate bedroom and sitting room provide the housekeeper her own space away from the guests while insuring her availability to respond when needed. The bathroom facilities include a large stall shower with grab bars for appropriate safety. The apartment is carpeted throughout and we are told repeatedly that it is attractive and comfortable.

Even persons living at home may require more attention than can be provided by a housekeeper. Behavioral problems including unsafe ambulation, or issues like the administration of medications, may require the presence of professional staff. These services are regulated by the licensure of agencies. Some liberalization of these requirements can be seen in the Senior Citizens Independent Community Care Act but this program is not expected to be more than experimental for some time (U.S. Senate, 1984). Since these are the services regularly provided in the nursing home, when space is available, respite is also provided in the SNF. Private rooms in the SNF provide respite patients the opportunity to live in a fully supported environment without the need to adjust to a room-mate in a limited stay situation. This approach to respite provides the family with the assurance that their loved one is fully cared for and protected during his/her stay with the Center.

The proximity of the two alternatives enables the Center to develop a range of services relative to the specific needs of clients. Meals may be taken in either location depending on the needs of the guest. For example, a guest requiring kosher meals can be provided for in the apartment by the utilization of frozen kosher meals, adequate planning and the cooperation of the family. Generally, it is advantageous for guests to take some meals in the SNF. This assures that they are ambulated and provides useful socialization for stimulation and orientation.

Additional socialization is provided by the activities program of the SNF. Intellectual stimulation, religious services, craft activities as well as regular social exchange with residents of the SNF, staff and volunteers ensure the availability of a program of services which can be tailored to the individual needs of each respite guest.

Developing a respite program in conjuction with an SNF provides for the availability of a variety of professional services and consultants. Nurses and social workers assess potential guests for their suitability for respective services. Dieticians assist in the development of menus for special needs or preferences as well as the necessary delivery of food to the apartment for both guests and the housekeeper. The personnel coordinator arranges for the housekeeper and additional aides, as well as the supplies needed to maintain and operate the apartment. The Social Service Department takes the initial inquiry, schedules respite placements, maintains liaison with families and the Westchester Chapter, A.D.R.D.A. as well as assuring proper notification to all those who will be involved in the placement. The Business Office including administration and bookkeeping maintains the financial records and arranges payment for the services. The Westchester Chapter, A.D.R.D.A. participates with families in the payment of services on a sliding scale basis.

EVALUATING THE EXPERIENCE

It may be premature to indicate the success or failure of this respite service, but it is not too early to identify the criteria by which it should be judged. The development of this project is still taking shape. With each definition of objectives, criteria are identified by which to evaluate the project's success. The first criterion is the effectiveness of the assessment of potential clients. The program will not work if the client selection process cannot anticipate the ability of the guest to meet the expectations of placement. Since there is limited flexibility in placement services with SNF beds usually unavailable, the placement has to work. Therefore, assessment has to include meaningful levels of functioning and an effective way of accurately determining the client's capabilty.

The experience of the SNF in working with demented patients has produced a rating of cognitive ability and the skill necessary to apply this rating with consistent success (Miller, 1979). The major difficulty which sometimes invalidates this assessment is the presence of a functional mental health problem. Since many Alzheimer's patients have functional problems in addition, this could be a limiting factor in the success of this project.

Mentally ill patients may present themselves as demented. The incident mentioned earlier in the apartment project was such a case and points to the need for clear and effective communication and cooperation between the family care-givers and the respite project. In this case the client had recently moved in with the family. The family was looking to the patient's age as a justification for her behavior and was actively denying the presence of mental illness. The Center was quite fortunate in having a skilled bed available when the woman began to act out in the apartment with only an unskilled housekeeper in attendance.

The care-receiver was a woman whose husband had died six years earlier leaving her separated from her family in a Florida community. She had been an active woman socially but dependent on her husband for many instrumental activities, particularly in areas of decision making. Her son, an only child, saw his mother in ways that met his needs, i.e., as a socially effective, fun loving person. His wife saw her in more realistic terms, but was unwilling to get involved. It appeared as if the daughter-in-law understood and was reluctant to become responsible for her mother-in-law. When the husband was ill, prior to his death, the client's younger sister moved in with her to help her through a prolonged depression. In an interview the younger sister stated, "She was mean, selfish and abusive. She almost destroyed my life, I had to leave."

Through family interview, it was suggested that there had been a long history of psychopathology prior to and after the death of the husband. The clinical picture painted by the client's family was that of longstanding narcissism, manipulation, paranoia, bizarre behavior under stress, which included her sister's testimony that she was indeed addicted to barbituates. The grandchildren, when they had visited their grandmother in Florida, would come home to describe her bizarre behavior. In their words. "Grandma's off the wall." When the son would call his mother, her social affect would dissuade his fears and he would continue to see his mother in a way that met his needs. Even after the extended family interviews, where he was a regular participant, he was still finding it difficult to accept the fact that his mother was mentally ill.

The incident which had precipitated the son bringing his mother back to New York was an overdose of sleeping pills. The diagnosis on admission was hypertension and organic brain syndrome. After two months of working with this client, including regular sessions with a consulting clinical social worker, it became increasingly apparent that the level of dementia was minimal while the pychopathology that precipitated admission was manic-depressive illness with psychosis. The original evaluation had confirmed a moderate level of dementia illustrating the difficulty in diagnosing dementia of the Alzheimer's type as well as the need for an openness between families and providers of respite services.

In addition to a specified level of cognitive ability, clients for the apartment need certain skills in their activities of daily living (ADL), and the ability to ambulate safely (Spence & Brownell, 1984). Each guest must be able to get up and use the bathroom if necessary during the night without risk of falling. The skills required to effect these behaviors and others required in the relative independence of the apartment again emphasize the need for effective cooperation with family caretakers. It is not uncommon to find that family members would like to think that their loved one is less disabled than he/she really is (Miller & Harris, 1976).

The place of the primary care-giver is critical in a program of respite services. This is the second criterion in evaluating the respite project. The primary care-giver is the focus of the delivery of service although not the recipient of care. What little data are available indicate the positive response to the relief of care-giving with less than 2 percent of primary care-givers indicating any dissatisfaction. At the same time, if one looks at outcome as a function of the status of the care-receiver, 22 percent are in worse condition one month after than they were before the experience. Care-receivers whose condition declined are generally those who had a "short" stay (the Foundation for Long Term Care, 1983). It is probably that care-receivers suffer from the trauma of relocation (Spence and Cunningham, forthcoming), with little chance of working through an effective adjustment in a less than three week period. If the primary care-giver fails to recognize this before the placement and the care-receiver does respond poorly, chances are the placement will be viewed as unsatisfactory. This may be why 17 percent of those reporting in The Foundation for Long Term Care report indicate that they would not use respite again (p. 20).

The adjustment of a care-receiver is influenced significantly by their relationship to the housekeeper/companion. This third criterion is critical but a dificult one to control given the relatively low pay provided and the subsequent lack of training that one can expect of someone in this position. The desired qualities of a person for this post would be a mature, responsible individual with good judgment who is outgoing and friendly, well organized in her work and flexible enough to be able to adapt to changing clients with varied needs and tastes. The fact that the apartment provides the housekeeper with a comfortable home on a continuing basis is a built-in bonus. When there are periods without clients in the apartment the person fills in as an aide in the SNF thereby adding to her training experience in working with the ill aged. The Center has had some difficulty in finding the right person for this position.

The final criterion that must be encompassed in an evaluation of the project is the perspective of the Center. It is not a profitable undertaking. The labor costs alone are more than the daily rate for the apartment. Respite in the SNF is discounted slightly from the regular continuing placement rate as a courtesy to the Westchester Chapter, A.D.R.D.A. at a level slightly better than break even. Meeting a genuine need in the community is the major motivation for the Center. The goodwill generated therefrom is, of course, dependent on people viewing the respite program as a community service. If it works, the Center benefits by being viewed as contributing to community needs by delaying or preventing institutionalization, as a facility appropriate for long-term patients when they need skilled care, and as a potential recipient for gifts and bequests in support of Center programs. So far this has demonstrated itself in that three of the ten clients that have used the service are now long-term residents in the SNF and one family has made a contribution to the Center in the name of their relative.

Respite is perceived as one of a continuum of services to be provided by the Nathan Miller Center. These services will include long-term home health care, residential and institutional respite and long-term nursing home care. To paraphrase the late Dr. E. M. Bluestone, the real challenge will be to provide the right service to the right client at the right time at the right price.

As Robert Morris (1981) has indicated, social policy with respect to the responsibility of needed services is undergoing significant change. Fedreal responsibilities which once included group identified needs to improve the quality of life for frail, chronically ill older people are being shifted to state and local governments as well as to the private sector. If families are to play any significant role in caring for Alzheimer's patients there will be a growing need for respite services. Policy which will determine and support services need to be based on the experiences of a full range of family circumstances. This paper and the program it describes have identified some of the conceptual problems that will need consideration if these policies are to serve family care-givers in a cost effective way and not just satisfy the vested interests of specific population segments.

REFERENCES

Carter, J. (1981). Day Services for Adults. London: George Allen & Unwin.
Eggert, G.M., Bowlyou, J.E., & Nichols, C.W. (1980). Gaining control of the long term care system: first returns from the Access experiment. The Gerontologist, 20:356-363.
Estes, C.L. (1979). The Aging Enterprise. San Francisco: Jossey-Bass.
Hodgson, J.H. & Quinn, J.L. (1980). The impact of the Triage health care delivery system on client morale, independent living and the cost of care. The Gerontologist, 20:364-371.

Liddiard, R. (1980, April). Presentation to AoA long-term care delegation on geriatric medicine in Scotland, England, Norway and Sweden.

Miller, M.B. (1979). Variants of the Clinical Syndrome of Organic Brain Disease, In Miller, M.B. *Current Issues in Clinical Geriatrics.* New York: The Tiresias Press, pp. 187-203.

Miller, M.B., Bernstein, H. & Sharkey, H. (1979). The "missing parent"—institutional rediscovery. In Miller, M.B. *op. cit.* pp. 29-62.

Miller, M.B. & Harris, A.P. (1976). Family cognizance of disability in the aged on nursing home placement. In Miller, M.B. *The Interdisciplinary Role of the Nursing Home Director.* Wakefield, MA: Contemporary Publishing, pp. 172-185.

Miller, M.B. & Harris, A.P. (1976). The Chronically ill aged: paradoxical patient-family behavior. In Miller, M.B. *op. cit.* pp.167-171.

Morris, R. (1981) Forward. In Frankfather, D.L. et al. *Family Care of the Elderly.* Lexington, MA: D.C. Heath.

Perdue, Joanne (1984). Respite care for the frail or disabled elderly. *Pride Institute Journal of Long Term Home Health Care.* 3:31-43.

Spence, D.L. & Brownell, W.W. (1984). Functional assessment of the aged person. In Granger, C.V. & Gresham, G.E. (Eds.). *Functional Assessment in Rehabilitation Medicine.* Baltimore, MD: Williams & Wilkins, pp. 254-272.

Spence, D.L. & Cunningham, J.J. (In press) Social factors and family supports. In Calkins, E. (Ed.). *The Practice of Geriatric Medicine.* Philadelphia, PA: W.B. Saunders.

The foundation for long term care (1983). *Respite care for the frail elderly.* Albany, NY: The Center for the Study of Aging, Inc.

U.S. Senate Special Committee on Aging (1984). *Developments in Aging 1983.* Washington, D.C.: USGPO.

U.S. Senate Special Committee on Aging (1982). *Developments in Aging 1981.* Washington, D.C.: USGPO.

WORLD OF PRACTICE

A Model for Family Meetings in the Long Term Care of Alzheimer's Disease

Kathy J. Fabisewski, RN, CMS
Mary C. Howell, MD, PhD

ABSTRACT. The progressive intellectual, behavioral and functional deterioration characteristic of Alzheimer's Disease, ultimately necessitates institutionalization. Not only do families of these patients experience intense feelings of grief, anger, and sadness but additionally must cope with the enormous formerly-shared stresses of legal problems, economic management and family negotiations. There is a need for knowledge about the disease process, opportunity to ventilate feelings and concerns, and guidance in the decision-making process with regards to the level of medical intervention at the time of a life-threatening illness. A model for periodic family conferences with the long term care multidisciplinary treatment team, to meet the unique needs of family members of institutionalized Alzheimer's Disease patients is described.

Alzheimer's Disease is an idiopathic, progressive neurological disorder characterized by the syndrome of intellectual deterioration, disorganization of the personality and inability to carry out the normal tasks of daily living.[1] Caring at home for a patient with global losses in cognitive and behavioral function is a struggle. In addition,

---

Kathy J. Fabisewski, 9 Fairmount Street, Salem, MA 09170.

the inevitable institutionalization that this irreversible disease ultimately warrants can precipitate a crisis of individual and family disorganization. It is stressful and depressing for family members to lose a formerly stable member;[2] in addition, chronic and debilitating illness disrupts established roles within the family as a unit. Change and reorganization are necessary for the group to regain its equilibrium.[3] Families of institutionalized patients with the severe functional and physical impairments found in moderate to advanced Alzheimer's Disease present a particularly challenging problem for health professionals. Family members need knowledge about the disease process and its complications, opportunities to ventilate personal feelings and concerns, and guidance in the process of making decisions about care. The latter issue is inevitably focussed on the question of how much high-technological intervention should be used in the event of life-threatening acute illness or cardiopulmonary arrest.

At the ENRM VA Hospital in Bedford, Massachusetts, meeting the psychosocial needs of the family with regard to their relationship to, and care of, the patient with Alzheimer's Disease is seen as a primary obligation of patient care. The Geriatric Research, Education and Clinical Center (GRECC) includes a 46-bed diagnostic and treatment unit devoted to the development and evaluation of innovative approaches to patient-care management in Alzheimer's Disease. One of our major goals is to facilitate understanding of the complex medical, economic and psychosocial needs of the families of our patients. Our multidisciplinary treatment team, comprised of a physician, nurse practitioner, nursing unit administrator and social worker, recognizes that patients and their families must be considered as dynamic units and dependent one on the other. In most cases families of our patients kept their loved one at home for as long as they were able to manage his care. When long-term (permanent) admission of their spouse, sibling or significant other inevitably becomes medically and functionally necessary, a sense of personal tragedy is heightened for the family. At this time the intervention of the multidisciplinary treatment team can promote a trusting and resourceful long-term therapeutic relationship that offers a variety of help to families, both as collections of individuals and as interrelated groups.

A model for routine, periodic family conferences has been established. The conferences are designed to promote assessment of family structure and needs, teaching about the course of the disease as well as possible causes and the probable prognosis, and assistance · and support in the process of making decisions about on-going and anticipated modes of care. Families are enabled to participate in the planning and provision of treatment regimens. It is also useful to take opportunity in these family meetings to offer assistance to the family in evolving guidelines for direct-care staff with regard to the specific degree of medical intervention in the event of life-threatening illness. At every instance family members are encouraged to recognize and name their own very intense feelings of grief, anticipatory mourning, anger and sadness.

One recurring theme in these conferences is the need of family members for confidence in the positive regard of the caregivers for the patient. Discussion usually ranges over the provision of basic needs—nutrition, skin care, ambulation, recreation, bathing, grooming and toileting, for instance. Changes in techniques of care, including changes in medications, are fully discussed. For example, some family members may interpret patients' weight loss as inadequate nurturing,[4] and it is important to help them understand how this problem accompanies certain stages of the disease. There are also opportunities to discuss what are considered more discrete areas of concern, such as the shame and embarrassment they feel about the patients' loss of social skills. Again, it is important that they hear that these behaviors are part of the disease over which they have no control, so that their shame is lessened.

The loneliness and isolation experienced by family members—especially spouses—is consistently apparent. Many speak of confusion in social roles: are they still married, or widowed, or at some unnamed position in between? They are struggling to cope with responsibilities formerly shared with the patient, and coping as well with enormous stresses in the realms of legal problems, economic management, home maintenance, family negotiations, and so on. The team is alert to their needs for guidance, support and positive reinforcement of their coping skills.

In working with the adult children of patients with Alzheimer's Disease, issues of previous neglect and abuse by the affected individuals often are signaled by a striking ambivalence: the formerly abused child simultaneously expresses negative feelings, usually muted, with regard to the patient's earlier life, and at the same time is firmly reluctant to authorize limited comfort-and-support care for life-threatening symptoms. These adult children are often driven to demand the most elaborate technological care, aimed at preserving the patient's life without regard to questions of quality of existence. They seem unable to release the patient into a peaceful death without the interference of cardiopulmonary resuscitation and the assistance of complicated machinery such as ventilators and cardiac monitors.

Other essential topics, which we have come to see as integral components of our periodic family meetings, include early introduction of the questions of cardiopulmonary resuscitation and of transfer of the patient to an acute care ward such as an ICU. Few topics in medical care are more complicated, controversial and emotionally-charged than that of the treatment of the incurably ill.[5] We have found that the problem is more manageable when the families (who usually have legal guardianship, once patient incompetence is recognized) are informed of the ultimate course of the disease process. It is important to raise these issues at each meeting, giving full opportunity for each person in attendance to ask questions and ventilate feelings. We convey the expectation that in the long run we hope all family members can come to a consensus, but along the way it is essential that room for different opinions be permitted. We also recognize that a final decision about level of medical intervention can only be made at the moment of the acute—life-threatening—illness, and that before that time comes family members may very well shift in their opinions, reversing earlier decisions and re-assessing their own feelings. Although in a practical sense, on the ward, decisions about level of intervention will be made by the physician with ward responsibility at the moment, it is of great value to have documented in the chart the deliberations and preferences of family members.

It is our belief that this model for periodic family conferences facilitates establishment of the basic human premise of trust and better assists the multi-disciplinary team in understanding and meeting the unique needs of family members of institutionalized patients with Alzheimer's Disease.

REFERENCES

1. Hayter, Jean, Helping Families of Patients with Alzheimer's Disease, *Journal of Gerontological Nursing,* 8: 81-86, February, 1982.
2. Dietsche, I.M. et al., Alzheimer's Disease: Advances in Clinical Nursing, *Journal of Gerontological Nursing,* 8: 97-100, February, 1982.

3. Wanzer, Sidney H., M.D., The Physician's Responsibility Toward Hoplessly Ill Patients. *New England Journal of Medicine,* 310: 955-959, April 12, 1984.
4. Glaze, Bobbie, One Woman's Story, *Journal of Gerontological Nursing,* 8: 67-68, February, 1982.
5. Beam, Ida Marlene, Helping Families Survive, *American Journal of Nursing,* 2: 228-232, February, 1984.

BOOK REVIEWS

INSTITUTIONAL CARE OF THE MENTALLY IMPAIRED ELDERLY. J. S. Edelson and W. H. Lyons. *Van Nostrand Reinhold Co., New York, 1985, 219pp.*

Concern about shaping our programs to preserve or create life-enhancing environments for the elderly should make gerontology practitioners aware of their responsibility in shaping the institutional environment of long-term care settings, according to the authors of this book. The book, *Institutional Care of the Mentally Impaired Elderly*, attempts to shape, in a very practical way, the institutional environment. The basic premise of the book rests upon seeing the world through the eyes and minds of the mentally impaired, and as experienced by those who provide their care.

The book is based upon the experiences of the Jewish Home for the Aged in Toronto. The Home is one of a multi-service complex which provides a continuum of care for the aged, known as the Baycrest Centre for Geriatric Care. The book assembles the results of two government demonstration projects which were funded to enhance the environment of the institutional setting for the mentally impaired. A recurring theme found in the book's chapters is that there is an interdependence between the environment of the institution and the resident's behavior. The chapters provide many fine illustrations of care and techniques used with problem behavior residents, which not only altered the behavior of the resident in question, but more importantly, the attitude of the staff providing care.

The book is divided into five units. The first, Individualizing Nursing Care, contains four chapters. The first illustrates many basic intervention techniques for the care of the mentally impaired and outlines the practitioner's need for understanding the resident's motivation and meaning behind certain behaviors. This chapter provides excellent examples of actual experiences that are used to illustrate the approach of the authors to enhance and alter institutional environments. The second chapter illustrates the many approaches used to change the behaviors discussed in the first chapter. Some specific illustrations provided concern bathing, incontinence, agitated behaviors, accidents and the use of restraints. While the chapter is geared to the nursing profession, the illustrations and principles discussed are relevant to all professionals and para-professionals working in institutional settings.

The third chapter of the first unit describes the Centre's application of reality orientation as a tool for communication and training for both staff and residents. It is a well-developed chapter outlining the basic principles of the approach and some interesting uses of R.O. with families and direct service staff. The last chapter of this unit concerns itself with the organization of nursing care, and describes specific situations common in institutional settings—staff burnout, staff turn-over, area assignments, and the role of the charge nurse. Again, this chapter is geared to the nursing profession, but I found many points relevant to all who work in such settings.

The second two chapter unit describes specific activity programs implemented at the Home. The first chapter discusses the value of activity programming for residents and staff, and does a fine job of outlining basic principles of programming. The second chapter describes and discusses one such program, the women's club group. The principles described and the illustrations provided in this chapter are worthwhile to all who engage in group work with elderly people. This chapter compares well with the excellent works on group work by Saul and by Burnside currently available.

The third unit is devoted to the role of volunteers in an institutional setting. It provides excellent illustrations and practical applications for volunteers in such settings. This chapter will be worthwhile for all who use volunteers or wish to utilize volunteers in their programs.

The fourth unit of the book deals with the role of the family in institutional care. It describes the role of the family in decision making about insititutionalization and in the continuing care of the resident. It also provides an excellent description of how staff can help families in accepting institutional placement and in visiting with their loved one.

The final unit outlines several institutional challenges including treatment teams, evaluation and assessment of care, and staff development. The authors point to the continuing challenge of discovery in institutional care of the mentally impaired.

The book is focused on how the care situation is perceived and experienced by the mentally impaired resident, his or her family, and the direct care staff. It concentrates its attention on the psycho-social aspects of institutional care, because it is within this realm that the quality of life issues are measured. The book elucidates ways of viewing situations rather than giving a set formula for solutions to situations, and this is perhaps, one of its best qualities. The authors illustrate problem areas with actual case studies and incidents, and apply many principles and practices to these. No one solution is presented, but a number of possibilities are presented for the reader to explore.

The book is well-written and organized. It concentrates its efforts at the mentally impaired elderly, but it is of use to all who work in the field of aging, not just institutional settings. The book seems to be written with the nursing profession in mind, however, it is applicable to all practitioners in the field. The main points of the book, recognizing the environmental impact on resident behavior, role of family and volunteers, activities programming and other approaches to the continuum of care in an institution are all worthwhile, and of use to gerontology practitioners and students.

Robert A. Famighetti
Assistant Professor and
Director of Gerontology
Kean College of New Jersey
Union, NJ 07083

ALZHEIMERS'S DISEASE AND RELATED DISORDERS: RESEARCH AND MANAGEMENT. W. E. Kelly, editor. *Charles C. Thomas & Co., Springfield, IL, 1984, 215pp., $29.95 (cloth).*

During the past few years increasing attention to the understanding of Alzheimer's Disease, a major health problem of the 1980s, has taken place. Several noteworthy books, such as those by Mace and Rabins *(The 36-Hour Day)* and Powell and Courtice *(Alzheimer's*

Disease: A Guide for Families) have focused attention on the family caretaking issues, and offer much needed advice and information about the disease to families. The topic of Alzheimer's disease has become one of major social and professional concern.

This edited volume by William Kelly, *Alzheimer's Disease and Related Disorders: Research and Management,* offers a professional and medically oriented approach to the topic. Based on the proceedings of a seminar organized by the Veterans Administration and the Thomas Jefferson University School of Medicine, this collection of papers presents the state of the art regarding diagnosis, assessment, treatment, and research on Alzheimer's and Related Disorders.

Given the sophistication of many of the chapters, the book is primarily seen as useful for those already knowledgeable about the disease or working in the field, and provides greater insight to existing research findings. The book attempts to offer clarity to three main themes about the disease. First, to examine the enormity of the problem of these disorders and the social and public policy dilemmas presented by such disorders. Several chapters provide an excellent review of these issues including the chapter by Gurland which examines the epidemiology of the disease, and the chapter by Mahairas that reviews the current social and public policy issues confronted by the disease.

The second main theme to the book is the growing awareness that Alzheimer's disease may be a disorder of acetylcholine metabolism in the brain. This recent and exciting discovery is discussed in two chapters. It is examined in the chapter by Cohen as he presents an overview of the current level of knowledge and research on the research, practice and policy issues of the disease. The topic is more fully explored in the chapter by Price who heads the research team doing this research.

The third major theme explored by the book deals with the problem of diagnosis. Dr. Randels presents a thorough examination of the problems with diagnosis and errors regarding dementia, pseudodementia, and depression in the elderly.

After an initial overview chapter by Cohen, the book divides into two discrete sections. In the first section, Richard Mohs presents a comprehensive and thorough review of existing research on the topic. Randel, in another chapter, provides important insight into electro-physiological research and the current search for biological markers for these diseases. These chapters emphasize the need for early detection and present an optimistic outlook for intervention and treatment.

Price et al., in chapter five, outline their discoveries about the neuropathology of the plaques found in the cerebrum of Alzheimer's victims. In the chapter by Sinex and Kraus, they propose that Alzheimer's disease is genetic and suggest a hypothesis that includes an altered purine biosynthesis. Their approach to the disease's cause is based on the fact that most people with Down's Syndrome, who live long enough, also get Alzheimer's Disease.

The second section of the book deals with specific treatment modalities for Alzheimer's victims and their families. Mahairas, for instance, confronts the issues associated with reimbursement and adequate care facilities available to those suffering from the disease. Barry Gurland and his colleagues reviews the incidence, distribution, socio-cultural influences, and social supports available for this disease, and forecast a significant increase in the incidence of the disease based upon their data.

Paul Haber's chapter provides an overview of the extensive medical care programs and initiatives being implemented by the Veteran's Administration. The future problem facing the Veteran's Administration as the number of aging veterans increases is excellently outlined and discussed.

The chapter by Kennedy and Deikis outlines the problem that psychologists face in using current psychologial tests to diagnose Alzheimer's disease and related disorders. This chapter emphasizes the dilemmas faced by testing and diagnosis of the diseases. Nancy Mace's chapter provides both informative and practical information to family caretakers, and describes a program for self-help family support groups.

The book ends with a panel discussion by the conference's seventeen presenters and their interaction with members of the invited audience. The book also contains an excellent appendix for the organization of a twenty-bed care unit for Alzheimer patients.

The chapters of the book are well-written, comprehensive in scope and informative, despite some intended overlap between chapters. The book is most useful for medical practitioners and nursing home personnel. It's level may be too advanced for the layperson, but even family members interested in the current medical research being conducted and the various dilemmas raised

by this research will find the book worthwhile. Unlike the books by
Mace and Rabins and Powell and Courtice mentioned previously,
this book has a somewhat more limited appeal, but is still worthwhile
reading.

Robert A. Famighetti
Assistant Professor and
Director of Gerontology
Kean College of New Jersey
Union, NJ 07083

ALZHEIMER'S DISEASE: A GUIDE FOR FAMILIES. Lenore
S. Powell and Katie Courtice. *Addison-Wesley Publishing Co.,*
Reading, MA, 1983, 277 pp.

Alzheimer's disease has been receiving an increasing amount of
attention not only by gerontologists but also by other professionals
in human services. As the elderly population in our society increases
and as more attention is paid to the problems of the aging population, greater numbers of Alzheimer victims have been identified.
Like many other mental disorders, Alzheimer's is a family illness
and the entire family has to be involved in the disease and its treatment.

The authors have set out to write the definitive work on this illness for those people they have identified as caregivers, namely, the
extended family. They have been, for the most part, successful.
Their explanations and descriptions of the causes and courses of this
illness are well done and easily understood by the lay person. If they
can offer little hope for the current sufferers, they are quick to spell
out the areas of research that are now being undertaken. The more
information and understanding a caregiver has, the better they will
be able to cope with the afflicted family member.

When the authors begin to discuss the caregiver's anger, frustration, denial, depression and guilt, the discussion is confusing and
often difficult to follow. Rather than providing a guide to aid the
caregiver in coping with these inevitable reactions to the Alzheimer

victim's disease, the discussion contributes little understanding to what we know about these human reactions from other sources.

The authors chose to include several exercises for use by the caregivers for their own self-preservation, i.e., relaxation and stress-reduction exercises. The idea is excellent, but so loosely developed and described as to be useless.

With these one or two exceptions, the main premise of this book is well met. The caregiver is provided with a great deal of factual information ranging from what to expect as the illness progresses, to the criteria for picking a good nursing home when the need arises. The caregivers are both cautioned and urged to take care of themselves throughout the exhausting ordeal of taking care of their needy relative. The description of the psychological toll that the caregiver undergoes is particularly beneficial. We are repeatedly reminded that the patient has no recollection of his behavior, however disruptive or upsetting. Those memories are left only for the caregiver who is very often devastated, angered or extremely hurt by the event. The addition of comments by other care-givers is a worthwhile addition to much of the text. They serve nearly the same function as a support group would—that of sharing experiences in dealing with the Alzheimer victim's symptoms.

The section on support groups is enriched by the valuable addition of an appendix of these groups in place around the country as of 1982. Again, in their zeal to share all of their knowledge, the authors get far too complex as they attempt to delve into comparisons of self-help groups with psychotherapy groups, thereby losing sight of Alzheimer's. A very brief description of psychotherapy and its advantages would have sufficed.

Much of what has been written up to this point relating to Alzheimer's disease has been of a scholarly nature, which although necessary, has been of little direct benefit to those of us who are directly involved in the day to day care of the impaired family member.

What emerges from this book is the extent of the devastation brought not only on the patient and the spouse, but on the entire family constellation. Very few of us have the financial means to hire the kind of trained assistance which would allow us a break in the total care necessitated by a severely impaired Alzheimer victim. Unless a close network of family and friends can be developed it is obvious that an even greater pressure will be exerted on already over-burdened nursing home facilities. As more and more victims are identified, communities of care providers will have to develop creative outlets to meet the needs of both patients and care providers. This volume could well be the first step in releasing those creative ideas by alerting lay readers to the shared concerns of all of us whether professional or family member who must deal with the victims of this very insidious disease.

Ruth Kaplan, ACSW
Director of Social Services
The Bridgeway
North Little Rock, AR 72118.